Personal Decision Making

FOCUS
on Economics

Don R. Leet

R. J. Charkins

Nancy A. Lang

Jane S. Lopus

Gail Tamaribuchi

OVER **45** YEARS
National Council on Economic Education
SINCE 1949

Economics America
National Council on
Economic Education

A partnership of education, business, and labor

AUTHORS

Don R. Leet, Chairman, Economics Department
Director, Center for Economic Education
California State University, Fresno

R. J. Charkins, Executive Director, **Economics**America of California

Nancy A. Lang, Director, Center for Economic Education
Northern Kentucky University

Jane S. Lopus, Director, Center for Economic Education
California State University, Hayward

Gail Tamaribuchi, Director, Center for Economic Education
University of Hawaii–Manoa

CONTENTS

FOREWORD

Personal Decision Making: Focus on Economics, a core volume in a new generation of National Council publications, is dedicated to increasing the economic literacy of *all* students. The *Focus* publications, the new centerpiece of **Economics**America, build on almost five decades of success in delivering economic education to America's students.

The *Focus* series is both new and innovative, using economics primarily to enhance learning in subjects such as history, geography, civics, and personal finance. Activities are interactive, reflecting the belief that students learn best through active, highly personalized experiences with economics. Applications of economic understanding to real-world situations and contexts dominate the lessons. In addition, the lessons explicitly teach the voluntary national standards in economics, outlined in the National Council's *A Framework for Teaching the Basic Economic Concepts.*

Personal Decision Making: Focus on Economics highlights and examines basic economic concepts as they relate to consumer, business, social, and personal choices. Students see connections between their classroom learning and their real-world experiences in budgeting, career planning, credit management, and housing. They learn that people will always have limited resources and relatively unlimited wants—the human condition called *scarcity.* Students discover that economics provides simple yet powerful tools to help people think critically about scarcity situations. And they learn how to use these tools to help them make decisions about how to prepare themselves for the world of work.

Michael Watts, Professor of Economics, Purdue University, and Senior Fellow, National Council on Economic Education, reviewed the manuscript and offered many valuable suggestions. The authors and the publisher are responsible for the final publication.

The National Council thanks the authors, Don R Leet, who took the lead on this project, and his coauthors: R. J. Charkins, Nancy A. Lang, Jane S. Lopus, and Gail Tamaribuchi for helping teach students to use economic tools in exciting and different ways to make decisions about personal finance. We recognize, as well, the financial support of the National Science Foundation.

Joan Sullivan Baranski
Publisher

ACKNOWLEDGMENTS

We acknowledge the help of the following teachers in reviewing and pilot testing the materials in *Personal Decision Making: Focus on Economics*.

Ann Boylan
Alvarado Middle School
Union City, California

Lewis Dunn
Edison High School
Fresno, California

Deborah J. Edwards
Simon Kenton High School
Independence, Kentucky

Dale Hammel
Hoover High School
Fresno, California

Lyle E. Hendricks
Farrington High School
Honolulu, Hawaii

Richard Higgerson
Alvarado Middle School
Union City, California

James Lloyd
Bullard High School
Fresno, California

Donna McCreadie, President
California Association of School Economics
Teachers
Temple City High School
Temple City, California

Gwen Maeda
McKinley High School
Honolulu, Hawaii

Rhonda Nagao
Castle High School
Kaneohe, Hawaii

Patricia Puckett
Alvarado Middle School
Union City, California

Tom Schaerges
Konocti Adult School
Lower Lake, California

Judy Shahenian
Mission San Jose High School
Fremont, California

Rudolph Shappee
Scripps High School
San Diego, California

Linda Taylor
Conner Senior High School
Hebron, Kentucky

Scott Thomas
Conner Senior High School
Hebron, Kentucky

David L. Vannasdall
Woodland Middle School
Taylor Mill, Kentucky

Sue Weaver, Secretary Treasurer
California Association of School Economics
Teachers
Ramona High School
Ramona, California

We also thank Rosella Banister, Director, National Institute for Consumer Education, for reviewing the entire manuscript and providing insightful comments. The staff at the National Council on Economic Education provided guidance and encouragement. We are especially grateful to S. Stowell Symmes for overseeing the project from its inception and to Robert Highsmith and Joan Sullivan Baranski for their encouragement and support.

INTRODUCTION

RATIONALE

When university professors of economics are asked what they hope to instill in their students once the students successfully complete an introductory course, the most common response is "an appreciation for the economic way of thinking." John Maynard Keynes, one of the most famous economists who ever lived, used a similar meaning when he defined economics as an "apparatus of the mind." The authors believe that studying economics is more than simply learning a body of received knowledge. Rather it is a matter of understanding economic concepts and being able to employ them in different situations.

This set of lessons in personal decision making was conceived with the idea that students could benefit significantly from learning to view problems from an economic point of view. What is an economic perspective? It begins with the realization that we will never have everything we want. We will always have limited resources and relatively unlimited wants. This is the human condition called *scarcity*. Economists see scarcity, choices, and decision making as the cornerstones of any problem-solving approach. We believe that economics has developed some simple but powerful tools for helping people think critically about scarcity situations. We also believe that people almost always have alternatives when confronted with scarcity. As the former chair of the economics department at Harvard University, James Duesenberry, once wrote: "Economics is all about how people make choices; sociology is all about how people have no choices to make."

RELEVANCE FOR THE WORLD BEYOND THE CLASSROOM

In *Personal Decision Making: Focus on Economics*, we use basic economic concepts to clarify common topics explored in a variety of high school courses that are intended to prepare students for the world of work. These courses have various titles such as: Consumer Economics, Introduction to Business, Introduction to Social Sciences, Sociology, Personal and Social Living, or something similar. The common theme in these courses is an attempt to connect students' learning with their real world experiences.

The topics selected are similar to those found in many high school courses. They include budgeting, career planning, credit management, and housing to name a few. There are several important differences between these lessons and those of a more traditional consumer-based curriculum.

SIX GUIDING PRINCIPLES FOR *PERSONAL DECISION MAKING: FOCUS ON ECONOMICS*

1. **Consumer Decision Making.** Many lessons focus on consumer choices. We look at common consumer topics such as Credit (Lesson 10), Housing (Lesson 11), and Personal Investments (Lesson 14). We believe that these will have relatively strong appeal for students who will be confronting such topics very soon. Our purpose is to improve student decision-making skills.

2. **Producers As Well As Consumers.** It is important for teenagers to appreciate their roles as producers as well as consumers. In order to have a high standard of living, students have to learn to be productive workers and entrepreneurs. Two early lessons (Lessons 2 and 3) explore goal setting and career planning to help students see that they can be successful in the economy if they plan carefully.

3. **Concerned Citizens.** Very few teachers will use *all* of these lessons, but we hope that the lessons involving personal choice with societal implications are taught. We have deliberately included some lessons that go beyond narrow self-interest. In Lesson 12 (Advertising) we encourage students to consider the larger question of the relationship between consumer sovereignty and advertising expenditures. We include a variety of opinions but leave the final decisions to the students. In Lesson 8 (Government) students learn about the broad range of services that government provides and try to tie their taxes to government's role in a modern economy.

4. **Other Points of View Important.** We try to help students see the logic of other people's perspectives. In the simulations we put the student

position of being an adult, whether the role [t]hat of a parent (Lesson 2), a business owner [L]esson 7), a politician (Lesson 8), a labor negotiator (Lesson 9), or an investor (Lesson 14). Students begin to see that adult decisions are generally based on the costs and benefits of their actions.

5. **A Limited Set of Concepts.** One objective of this program is to improve students' decision-making skills by concentrating their attention on a small set of economic concepts that promote "the economic way of thinking." We reinforce this theme by presenting students with a variety of scarcity situations where they need to apply the economic tools to reach a logical conclusion.

6. **Active Learning.** These lessons are as activity-oriented as possible. There are simulations, role plays, and small-group activities that require students to move around in the classroom and actively participate in the learning process. At times this can be a disadvantage if the location or the size of the classroom inhibits such active learning. We are confident that the teachers who are interested in these lessons will adapt them to suit their classrooms. We welcome comments and suggestions for future revisions.

ABILITY GUIDELINES AND FLEXIBILITY OF TEXT

Personal Decision Making: Focus on Economics is suitable for a wide variety of curriculum needs and teaching strategies. The lessons provide for great flexibility in teaching and learning–offering ample support for students of different ability levels. As there is no single approach or method adequate in all situations, the authors suggest many approaches for teachers to choose from to best suit the needs of their individual courses and to match the abilities, interests, and backgrounds of students. In general, the lessons are for all students.

KEY TO ABILITY LEVELS

The following coding system identifies activities suitable for students of various ability levels:
- ★ all students–basic course material
- ■ average and above average students

PLANNING CHART

This planning chart lists the six performance outcomes developed by the National Council on Economic Education. All lessons assist students in becoming more knowledgeable consumers, but each lesson emphasizes at least one other performance outcome. The chart should be especially helpful as educators begin to address the national standards in economics.

PLANNING CHART: CLASSIFICATION OF LESSONS BY PERFORMANCE OUTCOMES

Performance Outcomes	Lessons														
	1	2	3	4	5	6	7	8	9	10	11	12	13	14	15
Knowledgeable Consumers	X	X	X	X	X	X	X	X	X	X	X	X	X	X	X
Productive Workers		X		X			X		X						
Informed Citizens					X			X	X	X		X	X		X
Prudent Savers and Investors						X	X			X	X		X		
Effective Participants in the Global Economy															X
Lifelong Decision Makers	X	X	X			X				X	X		X	X	

LESSON 1
DECISION MAKING: SCARCITY, OPPORTUNITY COST, AND YOU

INTRODUCTION

The core concept in economics is *scarcity*, which results from the basic relationship between relatively unlimited wants and limited resources. Since we cannot have everything we want, we are forced to make choices. The concept of *scarcity* leads to decision making-situations at both personal and societal levels. Every choice involves a *trade-off*, that is, you must give something up if you want to get something. Whatever you give up is your *opportunity cost*. If you choose to use your resources in one way, then the real cost of that choice is the lost opportunity to use the resources in some other way. For example, at this moment you have chosen to use your time (a valuable resource) to read this lesson. Is there an opportunity cost to this time? Yes, another activity you would like to be doing now, but cannot, is your *opportunity cost*.

American consumers are constantly bombarded with "free samples" and "free prizes" as in "you have just won...." This lesson imitates the everyday phenomenon of "free" goods and illustrates that there is no such thing as a "free" lunch.

People make thousands of economic choices every year. By teaching students to understand the opportunity costs and weigh the consequences of the decisions they make, their actions will be more informed and prudent.

CONCEPTS

Scarcity
Opportunity cost
Trade-offs: Weigh costs and benefits
Consequences

CONTENT STANDARD

All decisions involve opportunity costs. Weighing the costs and benefits associated with alternative choices constitutes effective economic decision making.

OBJECTIVES

◆ Identify the opportunity cost in examples of personal decision making.

◆ Describe the trade-offs involved in their choices.

◆ Anticipate the consequences of their choices.

LESSON DESCRIPTION

Students participate in a group activity that illustrates the concepts of scarcity, opportunity cost, trade-offs, and consequences.

TIME REQUIRED

One class period.

MATERIALS

Gather five or six items that students consider valuable and different enough to be willing to weigh the costs and benefits of selecting just one. Some suggested items might be a homework pass, a get-out-of-quiz pass, an apple, a ticket to a school play, or athletic event, a library pass, a coupon for a 10-minute tutoring session, a school pin, a not-so-rare coin, a box of raisins, a healthful snack, a baseball card, a floppy disk, or a certificate for a free lunch with you. The one item that *must* be part of this simulation is a "free lunch" with the teacher.
★ Activity 1, Advice to the Sellers
★ Activity 2, Consumer Product Ranking Form
★ Activity 3, Franklin's Decision

PROCEDURE

1. Explain that this lesson helps students improve their decision-making skills. Students need to understand the meaning of "cost" as economists use the term. To an economist, even supposedly "free goods" can have significant costs.

2. Ask, "If I offer to give you something for nothing, is there a cost?" Allow some discussion

★ all students–basic course material
■ average and above average students

and do not debate the issue yourself. Restrict your remarks to clarifying the fact that you are going to give away some items today without asking for any money from the students.

3. Once the discussion has reached the stage where students understand they are going to receive "something for nothing" ask for volunteers to serve as sellers for each product. Select as many sellers as you have products to give away, but no fewer than four or more than six items. Explain that the remaining students will be consumers.

4. Give each volunteer seller one "free" item and a copy of Activity 1, Advice to the Sellers. Send students to the back of the room to read the copy and work on their presentations.

5. While the sellers are preparing, give each consumer a copy of Activity 2, Consumer Product Ranking Form, and remind them that today a variety of sellers will offer them "free samples" of their products. Each seller will have one minute to explain why consumers should prefer their product over all the others. After hearing all the sales pitches, each consumer will be asked to rank the samples, from the most preferred to the least preferred product, using the response form to record their preferences.

6. Invite sellers to sit in the front of the room and give them one minute each to promote their products. This should involve some humor and creativity on the part of the seller. Classroom appreciation should be enough incentive to bring forth clever presentations. It should not be necessary to provide a reward structure such as grade points for the presentation.

7. Choose the same number of consumers as there are sellers, choosing a replacement if a consumer fails to get a gift. Ask them to stand one at a time and state their selections in the order ranked. Ask sellers to stand in the order that consumers rank them. After each consumer has publicly ranked the items, ask the two questions in Step 8. Consumers must answer *both* correctly to get their highest ranked choice.

8. Consumers will receive the highest ranked

product only if they answer the following questions correctly. An incorrect response means the consumer does *not* get any item.

A. "Did your choice have a cost?"
    Correct Answer: Yes, an opportunity cost.

B. "What is the opportunity cost of your selection?"
    Correct Answer: The product ranked second (or the next available, if the second ranked has been taken by another consumer). This is their "opportunity cost" (lost opportunity) since by the rules of the game they could receive only one product. The "cost" of getting one product is not getting the second highest available alternative desired.

9. Repeat this process until there is only one item left. Keep that item for yourself.

10. Since consumers are supposed to rank the products according to their own tastes, there will usually be a change in the order sellers will stand and differing opportunity costs for consumers. Discuss these differences with student consumers who were not selected to publicly reveal their preferences.

11. After the buyers have received their products, pose the following question: "What positive or negative consequences might result from your selection?"

Possible Student Answers: A more pleasant personality, or weight gain and tooth decay from eating the snack; better grades with quiz exemption or from having lunch with the teacher, or discomfort from being called teacher's pet; happiness (disappointment) from seeing one's team win (lose) the athletic event; or lower grades if attending the game means less study time.

CLOSURE

Conclude the lesson by having the students review the opportunity costs and consequences illuminated in Activity 3, Franklin's Decision.

There are several ways to conduct this exercise. The simplest method would involve giving each student a copy of Activity 3 and, if time permits, having students share their answers.

A variation involves clustering the students after they select one of the options. Each cluster of students discusses their common option and selects a spokesperson to give their views. This could lead to a general discussion of the trade-offs they find acceptable for Franklin.

There are a variety of answers for some of the major consequences (both positive and negative) of each of these alternatives. For example:

Job Alternative: More income, a car, job experience, and larger savings are positive consequences; less study time, lower grades and consequently less chance for college scholarships or continuing education are negative consequences.

Football Team: New friendships and better health through exercise are positive consequences; lower grades, athletic injury, and lack of income are potential negative consequences.

Tutor Alternative: Some increase in income and higher grades may lead to academic success; not enough money for a car and fewer new friends might be some of the negative consequences.

ACTIVITY 1
ADVICE TO THE SELLERS

Name _____

Your job is to get the consumer to rank your product first, ahead of all the other products that will be sold in the classroom today. You are being given a few minutes to prepare your presentation now, but you will have only one minute to convince consumers that you have the best product. How do you do this?

1. Use a clever sales pitch. You are not supposed to lie, but you can use your imagination and honestly exaggerate why you believe your product will be of interest to consumers. After all, this is part of the reason advertising executives earn high incomes.

2. Emphasize how your product is used. Especially mention the many uses for your product that "ordinary" consumers might not see without your help.

3. Mention significant benefits that people gain by using your product. Try to make the consumers think they will get a great deal of satisfaction from using your product and must have it.

4. Tell why your product is the best. You may also want to mention some of the problems with your competitor's product, but be aware that this can lead to retaliation.

ACTIVITY 2
CONSUMER PRODUCT RANKING FORM

Name _____

Listen to several sales pitches made by your classmates who have products to give away. As you listen to each presentation, write the product name in the first column below and think about how much you would like to have that "free" product. After all sales presentations are completed, you will be asked to make a new list of the products advertised by ranking them according to how much satisfaction owning the product would give you. In the second column rate all the products offered by writing the product name you want the most at the top and the product you want the least at the bottom. You will be asked to reveal your preferences and, if you answer two questions correctly, you may receive what you want most.

<u>Product Names</u>
(gifts)

<u>Product Rankings</u>
(my preferences)

1._____

2._____

3._____

4._____

5._____

6._____

1._____

2._____

3._____

4._____

5._____

6._____

ACTIVITY 3
FRANKLIN'S DECISION

Name _____

Franklin is an eleventh grade student at Enterprise High. He is a solid B student with the following options:

Option I. Take a part-time job after school that pays minimum wage and requires him to work from 4:00 P.M. until 9:00 P.M. school nights. The extra money would allow him to buy a nice used car now, and he could save some money for college. On the other hand, his grades would suffer.

Option II. Join the football team which means he must practice every day after school. Franklin loves football. His coach thinks he has a good chance to get an athletic scholarship to a local college, but his mother is concerned about his grades. She is also worried about the possibility of his getting injured like his uncle who has bad knees as a result of playing professional football.

Option III. Study harder to improve his grades, and qualify as a "Student Tutor" in the after-school program. This would give him some spending money, and help him score better on the college entrance exams. Some of his teachers think he could get an academic scholarship if he spent his spare time studying. But tutoring would not give him enough income to get that used car.

Franklin has all of the standard teenage wants in alphabetical order: car, college, friends, money, and sports. In fact that's his problem. He can't do all three options at the same time. What should he do?

In order to help Franklin decide which alternative to choose, answer the following questions.

A. What are some of the major consequences (both positive and negative) of each of these alternatives?

Job Alternative:

Football Team Alternative:

Tutor Alternative:

B. Rank these options for Franklin from best to worst.

    1._____

    2._____

    3._____

C. Given these rankings, what is his opportunity cost?

D. List an important trade-off in Franklin's Decision.

E. How would you explain your decision to Franklin's mother?

LESSON 2
APPLYING A DECISION-MAKING MODEL: YOU AND YOUR FUTURE

INTRODUCTION

In Lesson 1 students explored the economic concepts of scarcity, trade-offs, and opportunity cost by creating a simulation involving "free" goods. The lesson concluded with Activity 3 that required students to apply these concepts to a decision by a hypothetical high school student, Franklin, who had to choose how to use his after-school time among three alternatives. This lesson builds on the previous lesson and introduces another tool, The Decision Grid, which uses the **PACED** decision-making model: *Problem, Alternatives, Criteria, Evaluation,* and *Decision* for student decision making.

CONCEPTS

Scarcity
Choice
Decision making
Alternatives
Criteria
Decision grid

CONTENT STANDARD

In our economic system, consumers, producers, workers, savers and investors seek to allocate their scarce resources to obtain the highest possible return, subject to the personal and institutional constraints of their situation.

OBJECTIVES

◆ Identify a scarcity situation.

◆ Differentiate between alternatives and criteria.

◆ Demonstrate the use of a decision-making grid.

LESSON DESCRIPTION

Students participate in a group activity using the decision-making grid. They learn why two individuals may reach different decisions even when they use an identical decision-making model. This lesson helps students appreciate different points of view.

TIME REQUIRED

One class period.

MATERIALS

★ Overhead transparencies of Activity/Visuals 1 and 2
★ Copies of Activity 1 for each cooperative learning group

PROCEDURE

1. Begin with a review of Franklin's Decision (Activity 3). Remind the class that Franklin was an eleventh-grade student who had three options. Ask students to give you those options orally. List the options on the chalkboard or on an overhead transparency. The options were:

> 1. Part-time job
> 2. Football team
> 3. Student tutor

2. After you list the options, put the word "alternative" above the list. Tell the class that each alternative is intentionally mutually exclusive. Franklin can choose only one alternative, he can't choose two. His problem is an economic problem. Because time resources are scarce he must give up something he wants to get his first choice. (Note: Many economic decisions we make are Franklin's kind of "all-or-nothing" choices; others we make permit us to do a little of one thing and a little of another; but even in these cases something is given up and the PACED model works for both.)

3. Next, ask the students to recall how they ranked these alternatives for Franklin. Select some students to respond to this question and have them briefly justify their answers. What were the reasons for their decisions? What was the *opportunity cost* of their decision? (*Answer:* the second ranked alternative. For example, if they ranked the student tutor option first, the job second, and football third, then the job was their opportunity cost—their forgone alternative).

4. Now tell the students that they are ready to learn a more systematic and thoughtful way to reach a decision, using a decision grid. Draw a grid around the alternatives already listed. Label the columns with the term, criteria.

ALTERNATIVES	CRITERIA		
Part-time job			
Football team			
Student tutor			

5. Define *criteria* as those personal goals that Franklin considers important. Remind students that a single goal is called a *criterion*. Illustrate the use of the grid by listing the goals that you believe Franklin values the most: he wants to attend college, spend time with school friends, and play sports. Place these criteria in the grid as shown here.

ALTERNATIVES	CRITERIA		
	COLLEGE	FRIENDS	SPORTS
Part-time job	+	−	−
Football team	+	+	+
Student tutor	+	−	−

6. Evaluate the alternatives according to each criterion. If the alternative helps Franklin to fulfill that goal, then place a + sign in the appropriate cell. Since a part-time job provides additional money for college, it gets a + sign. However, since this is an off-campus job, Franklin will have less time to spend with his friends. Thus we place a − sign in the friends column. Note that when evaluating the alternatives, not all criteria have to be weighted equally. We don't simply sum the plus and minus signs to make a decision. We assign relative importance to the different criteria. Weights can be illustrated by assigning double ++ or − − signs when evaluating alternatives against a particular criterion.

7. Divide the class into groups and give each group a copy of Activity 1. Tell students that they are to repeat the Franklin's Decision exercise, only this time they are to view Franklin's decision from *his mother's* perspective. Give them a few minutes to read the instructions and make their decisions.

8. While the students are filling in their decision grids, draw a blank grid on the chalkboard or put Visual 1 on the overhead projector. List Franklin's alternatives once again. Then, after most groups have finished, call on one group to place their criteria on the board. Have them place the plus (+) and minus (-) signs in each column. The finished grid might look like this:

ALTERNATIVES	CRITERIA		
	SAFE	SPENDING MONEY	COLLEGE SCHOLARSHIP
Part-time job	−	+	−
Football team	−	−	+
Student tutor	+	+	+

CLOSURE

Now that the class has had experience with using a decision-making grid, list the five-step decision-making model. Use Visual 2 and explain, using Franklin's Decision as an example.

Step 1. Define the *problem*.
For Franklin the problem was how to use his after-school time.

Step 2. List the *alternatives*.
There were three alternatives for Franklin: part-time job, football, or becoming a student tutor.

Step 3. Identify the relevant *criteria*.
These criteria were very different for Franklin and for his mother.

Step 4. Evaluate the *alternatives*.
This step allows you to compare the costs and benefits of each alternative regarding important goals.

Step 5. Make a *decision*.
As you saw from this exercise, Franklin's decision might be very different from his mother's because they had different criteria.

This model is sometimes referred to by an acronym, PACED, which highlights an important component in each step: *P*roblem, *A*lternatives, *C*riteria, *E*valuation, and *D*ecision.

Provide students with one or two copies of Activity 2 and ask them to use PACED decision making at least once during the next five days, when making personal, family, club or classroom decisions. Ask students to share their experiences at some future date.

ACTIVITY 1
FRANKLIN'S DECISION (FROM HIS MOTHER'S VIEW)

Name _____

Franklin is an eleventh-grade student at Enterprise High. He is the oldest child in a family of three (Franklin, his younger sister, and his mother). His mother is proud that he has a solid B average, but she does not like the fact that he played football on the junior varsity team last year. She does not think it is a very safe sport. She is constantly worried about the possibility of injury. Her brother has bad knees from his football playing days. She is also concerned about his safety if he works part-time at night, but she would like him to earn his own spending money so he could put something away for college. The family cannot afford to pay any college tuition. She would really like him to earn a college scholarship.

Option I. Take a part-time job after school that pays minimum wage and requires Franklin to work from 4:00 p.m. until 9:00 p.m. on school nights. The extra money would allow him to buy a nice used car now, and he could save some money for college. On the other hand, his grades might suffer.

Option II. Join the football team—this means he must practice every day after school. Franklin loves football. His coach thinks he has a good chance to get an athletic scholarship to a local college, but his mother is concerned about his grades. She is also worried about the possibility of his getting injured like his uncle who has bad knees as a result of playing professional football.

Option III. Study harder to improve his grades and qualify as a "Student Tutor" in the after-school program. This would give him some spending money and help him score better on the college entrance exams. Some of his teachers think he could get an academic scholarship if he spent his spare time studying. But tutoring would not give him enough income to get that used car.

1 What are the three alternatives for Franklin?
  1.
  2.
  3.

2. What are the three most important criteria to Franklin's mother?

  1.
  2.
  3.

3. In the grid shown evaluate the alternatives by placing a plus (+) or a minus (-) sign in each cell. Remember that you are looking at this decision from the mother's view.

ALTERNATIVES	CRITERIA		

VISUAL 1
A DECISION-MAKING GRID

ALTERNATIVES	CRITERIA			

VISUAL 2
FIVE-STEP DECISION-MAKING MODEL

Step 1.   Define The Problem.   **P**roblem

Step 2.   List Your Alternatives.   **A**lternatives

Step 3.   State Your Criteria.   **C**riteria

Step 4.   Evaluate Your Alternatives.   **E** valuation

Step 5.   Make A Decision.   **D**ecision

ACTIVITY 2
PACED DECISION MAKING

Name _____

The Problem _____

_____

_____

ALTERNATIVES	CRITERIA			

The Decision _____

_____

_____

LESSON 3
PLANNING AND GOAL SETTING: CAN YOU GET THERE FROM HERE?

INTRODUCTION

Goal setting helps people meet the challenges of today's world by providing them with targets to reach. People who have definite goals are more likely to get what they want out of life than those who do not set goals. Having goals influences how people make decisions and helps them develop plans of action to achieve their goals.

Our priorities influence our goals, what we do with our time, or even how we spend our money. We have many goals and limited time to accomplish them. Therefore, it is important that we develop a plan of action to help us achieve our goals.

CONCEPTS

Decision making
Opportunity cost
Scarcity
Choice
Alternatives

CONTENT STANDARD

All decisions involve opportunity costs; weighing the costs and benefits associated with alternative choices constitutes effective decision making.

OBJECTIVES

◆ Discuss and analyze the importance of goal setting.

◆ Determine how goal setting influences decision making.

◆ Apply the decision making grid to student goals.

LESSON DESCRIPTION

This lesson is in two parts. Part I focuses on how to set goals. Part II focuses on the influence goal setting has on exploring careers. Each part of the lesson can stand alone or can be used with Lesson 4, *A Student's Potential for the Labor Market* or Lesson 6, *Financial Planning: Budgeting Your Financial Resources*.

TIME REQUIRED

4 class periods (2 days Part I; 2 days Part II).

MATERIALS

★ Copies of Activities 1, 2, 3, and 4
★ Decks of Goal Cards for each group set up for Activity 1
★ Transparencies: Activity/Visual 1, 2 (optional)
★ Decision-making model (optional)

PROCEDURE

PART I: GOAL SETTING

1. Ask students, "Have you ever made a poor decision or a decision that you regretted?" Ask for a show of hands, then take a survey of the class. Tell students they are not unusual and that everyone has made a decision he or she regretted. Explain that this lesson will focus on goal setting and decision making.

2. In a large or small group setting, have students list possible reasons why they may have made poor decisions.

Possible answers might include: *the goal was no longer important to me, I didn't think it was going to be as difficult to accomplish the goal, or I decided to do other things.*

3. Place Visual 1, Goal Setting Process, on an overhead projector. Explain that the goal-setting process requires a clear focus. Setting goals helps people make decisions because they target or they identify the result they want from their decision. The goal-setting process includes the following: (1) reflect on and understand your priorities; (2) set a goal that is compatible with what you feel is important; (3) write your goal in a clear statement; (4) if necessary, divide your goal into manageable parts; (5) establish a timetable to accomplish your goal; and (6) make a commitment to accomplish the goal.

★ all students–basic course material
■ average and above average students

4. Explain that an action plan helps people achieve goals. A decision-making model is helpful in developing an action plan. It helps to identify what is important, where to start, what resources are needed, what the alternatives are, and how to evaluate the benefits and costs of each alternative.

5. Describe a scenario in which goal setting and decision making are important. For example: Susan is watching the Olympic figure skating competition on television. She decides her goal is to become an Olympic champion. (You can create another scenario that may better relate to the students in the class.)

6. In a small group setting, have students list and discuss what Susan must do to achieve her goals. If necessary, use transparency Visual 2, Decision-Making Model, to help students analyze Susan's dilemma.

Note: If students are unfamiliar with the decision-making grid and the PACED decision making model, introduce a lesson on its use before going on with this lesson. See Lesson 2.

State Susan's Goal: to become an Olympic figure skater

Define the Problem: need to develop an effective training program to become an Olympic figure skater

List Alternatives: train at home, train in another city

State Criteria: coaching, facilities, schooling, cost

Evaluate Alternatives: compare the costs and benefits of each alternative

Make a Decision: set a timetable to accomplish her goal

7. Discuss and list on the board decision-making situations in which goal setting is crucial. Examples: career planning, selecting a college, selecting courses to take, spending money, picking a mate, or saving or investing money.

8. Hand out Activity 1, Goal Setting Cards, and decks of goal cards to each group of students participating in this activity. Ask them to complete the activity as instructed.

CLOSURE

Summarize the criteria for goal setting and decision making. For an outside class activity, have students write down a goal they wish to accomplish before graduating from high school. Using a decision-making model, students are to develop action plans to help them achieve their goals. For each alternative listed, have students state the opportunity cost of each alternative. (Opportunity cost is the highest valued alternative that must be forgone because another option is chosen.)

PROCEDURE
PART II: EXPLORING CAREERS

This portion may be used alone or with Part I: Goal Setting. It may also be used with Lesson 4, *A Student's Potential in the Labor Market* and Lesson 6, *Financial Planning: Budgeting Your Financial Resources.*

1. Ask students to think about the following questions: "What kind of job do you want? What jobs are valuable to society? What jobs will you be good at and enjoy? Do you have the skills necessary for these jobs? What do you know about the jobs? How do your personal goals influence your career decisions?" If a student chooses homemaking or some other non-market activity, point out that this choice also involves an opportunity cost and the need for knowledge and preparation. Also note that non-market work can be very valuable to society even if it does not command a salary or wage.

2. Distribute Activity 2, Personal and Career Inventory, to survey students' interests, priorities and skills for various occupations.

3. After students have completed the survey, have them list two occupations to research. Distribute Activity 3, Career Planning Matrix.

Suggested Resources:
Occupational Outlook Handbook, (United States Department of Labor) gives descriptions, earn-

ings, working conditions, and employment outlook for more than 300 jobs. It is published
every year by the Bureau of Labor Statistics
and can be found at all public libraries and
most school libraries.

State Data Books

Periodicals: *The Wall Street Journal, National
Business Employment Weekly, Business Week,
Forbes, Fortune,* and others.

Professional organizations

4. After they complete Activity 3, ask students
to write a few paragraphs explaining the careers
they feel best support their interests, values, and
skills.

OPTIONAL ACTIVITY

Have students interview a person whose career
interests them. They may use Activity 4 as a
guide. After completing the interview, students
may make a short presentation about the person
they interviewed or write a short narrative about
the person. (These can be collected and used as
classroom resources.)

ACTIVITY 1
GOAL-SETTING CARDS

Name _____

Think about the future: How would you like your life to be two years out of high school? Five years out of high school? Ten years out of high school? Will you have completed your education? Will you be married? Will you have children? Will you be living in another city or state? Will you be living with your parents, in your own house, an apartment, townhouse, or condominium?

Directions:

1. Read each card in the deck.

2. Sort the cards into three piles:
   Pile 1: goals you want to accomplish
   Pile 2: goals in which you have no interest
   Pile 3: goals about which you are undecided

3. If you have more than 10 cards in pile one, re-sort the pile so you do not have more than 10 in pile one. Continue sorting until you are down to your top 10 goals.

4. Rank order the 10 goals (1 most important; 10 least important) you want to accomplish.

5. After you have ranked the goals in each pile, construct a chart of those goals you hope to accomplish in (1) two years after high school, (2) five years after high school, and (3)10 years after high school.

6. For each goal you have identified, list a short-term and a long-term action needed to attain the goal. Use the decision-making model to help you evaluate the actions needed to accomplish your goal. (This can be done individually or in groups of no more than three for obtaining other perspectives.)

GOAL CARDS

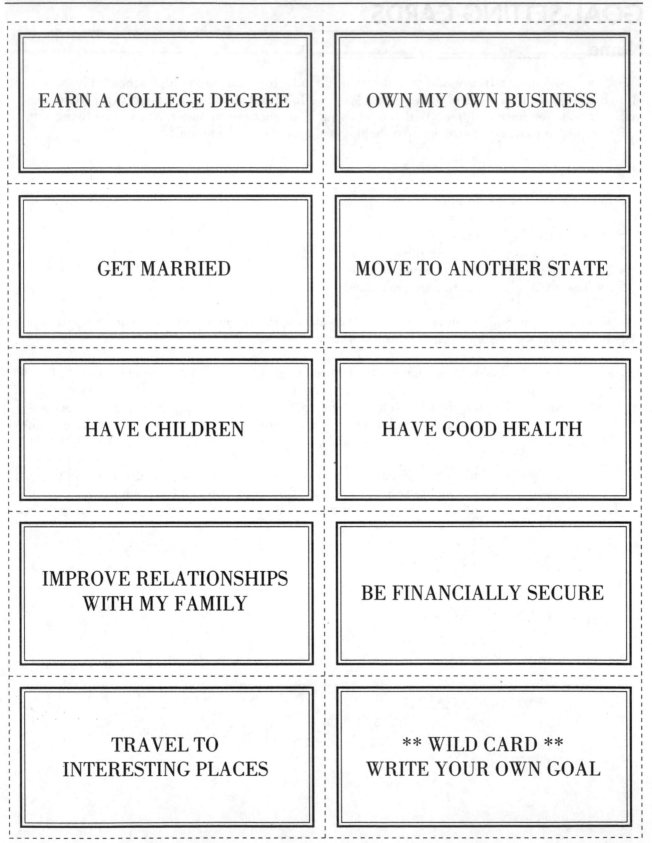

EARN A COLLEGE DEGREE	OWN MY OWN BUSINESS
GET MARRIED	MOVE TO ANOTHER STATE
HAVE CHILDREN	HAVE GOOD HEALTH
IMPROVE RELATIONSHIPS WITH MY FAMILY	BE FINANCIALLY SECURE
TRAVEL TO INTERESTING PLACES	** WILD CARD ** WRITE YOUR OWN GOAL

GOAL CARDS

LEARN TO FLY AN AIRPLANE	HAVE JOB SECURITY
LOSE WEIGHT	OWN A LUXURY CAR
BE MORE ASSERTIVE	LOOK ATTRACTIVE AND BE PHYSICALLY FIT
HAVE A FIRST CLASS SOUND SYSTEM FOR CAR OR HOME	HAVE MONEY TO INVEST
HAVE LOTS OF LEISURE TIME	BE RECOGNIZED AS AN EXPERT IN ANY FIELD

GOAL CARDS

BE ELECTED TO PUBLIC OFFICE	EXCEL IN A SPORT
HELP OTHERS LESS FORTUNATE THAN I	LIVE A LONG LIFE
BE AN ACTIVE MEMBER OF THE COMMUNITY	SAIL THE PACIFIC OCEAN
LISTED IN WHO'S WHO	BE AN ACTIVE MEMBER OF MY CHURCH
BUY A HOUSE	WRITE A BOOK

 From *Personal Decision Making: Focus on Economics,* © National Council on Economic Education, New York, NY

VISUAL 1
GOAL-SETTING PROCESS

1. Reflect on and understand your priorities

2. Set a goal that is consistent with what you believe is important

3. Write your goal in a clear statement

4. If necessary, divide your goal into manageable parts

5. Set a timetable for accomplishing your goal

6. Make a commitment to accomplish the goal

VISUAL 2
DECISION-MAKING MODEL

State Your Goal:

1. Define the Problem

2. List Alternatives

3. State Criteria

4. Evaluate Each Alternative

5. Make a Decision

ACTIVITY 2
PERSONAL AND CAREER INVENTORY

Name _____

Directions: Place an **X** over the number that shows how important you consider each value to be. Five is the highest and 1 is the least important value.

Working with people	1	2	3	4	5
Working with technical data	1	2	3	4	5
Working with ideas	1	2	3	4	5
Working with things	1	2	3	4	5
Working as part of a team	1	2	3	4	5
Working independently	1	2	3	4	5
Working regular hours	1	2	3	4	5
Changing working hours	1	2	3	4	5
Having variety on the job	1	2	3	4	5
Using current knowledge	1	2	3	4	5
Getting new skills/education	1	2	3	4	5
Achieving status or recognition	1	2	3	4	5

List two possible career areas that you might be interested in based on your answers to this inventory.

1. _____

2. _____

ACTIVITY 3
CAREER-PLANNING MATRIX

Name _____

Directions: Use available resources or other career information available to you to complete this survey. Select two careers that are of interest to you, fill in the information, and be prepared to discuss it with others.

FACTOR	CAREER 1	CAREER 2
Job title		
Description of work duties		
Starting salary/wage		
Salary range		
Education/training required		
Economic outlook in state/city		
Working conditions		
Career ladder		
Preparation for other jobs		
Advantages		
Disadvantages		
Does this career match your interests and skills?		

ACTIVITY 4
CAREER-PLANNING INTERVIEW

Name_____

Name of person interviewed _____

Title/position_____

Organization/company _____

Address _____

Telephone Number _____

Occupation _____

How long have you been in this occupation? _____

Describe a typical day at work (on other side of paper) _____

What do you enjoy most about your work? _____

What do you like least about your work? _____

What influenced you to choose this career? _____

What was your career path: education, training, previous work experience? _____

_____

What skills/competencies would be helpful to prepare for this occupation? _____

_____

What work schedule do you have?

a. Fixed hours or flexible _____

b. Average hours per day _____

c. Average hours per week _____

What is the average starting salary in this occupation? _____

What is the outlook for employment opportunities in this career in the future?_____

What advice would you give to students to make them more desirable to employers in this occupation?

_____

LESSON 4
A STUDENT'S POTENTIAL IN THE LABOR MARKET: IT'S A MATTER OF SUPPLY AND DEMAND

INTRODUCTION

One of the purposes of a high school education is to prepare students for the job market. In this lesson, students learn how the labor market determines wages. In applying the law of supply to the labor market, they see that workers are willing to supply greater quantities of labor at higher wages and smaller quantities of labor at lower wages. Similarly, in applying the law of demand to the labor market, students see that employers are willing and able to hire more workers at lower wages and fewer workers at higher wages. Together, the forces of supply and demand determine the wage in each type of labor market.

Different wages prevail in different labor markets depending upon the skills required for the jobs. Higher skilled jobs that are in demand command higher wages. Students complete a skills inventory and determine what steps they can take to improve their chances for success in the market economy.

CONCEPTS

Supply of labor
Demand for labor
Equilibrium wage
Skills

CONTENT STANDARD

Forces of supply and demand determine prices (wages), which are measures of the relative scarcity of different products (workers).

OBJECTIVES

◆ Use supply of labor and demand for labor to determine an equilibrium wage.

◆ Recognize that wages differ depending on supply and demand conditions in different markets.

◆ Perform a personal skills inventory to evaluate his or her potential in the labor market.

◆ Develop a plan to improve at least three skills.

LESSON DESCRIPTION

Students engage in two labor market simulations. One market is characterized by high wages and specific skill requirements; the other is characterized by low wages and low skill requirements. Students evaluate their own skills and plan ways to improve the skills in which they are weak.

TIME REQUIRED

Four class periods.
Period 1. Play the labor game.
Period 2. Discuss skills that will improve students' wage potential.
Period 3. Have students report on their plans for self-improvement.
Period 4. Have students bring in want ads related to two different labor markets.

MATERIALS

★ One set of white cards (26) for unskilled workers or workers whose skills are not in high demand and one set of blue cards (22) for employers of low skilled workers and workers whose skills are not in high demand. The appropriate number of cards at each wage should follow the supply and demand schedules in columns 1 and 2 in the tables in Activity 1. For example, there should be two white cards with a wage of $3.50, indicating two workers who would be willing and able to work at $3.50, and two white cards with a wage of $3.70. There should be one blue (employer) card with a wage of $5.30 and four blue cards with a wage of $3.50. Shuffle all decks.
★ One set of pink cards (22) for specific skilled workers and one set of green cards (28) for employers who need specific high skills. The appropriate number of cards at each wage should follow the supply and demand schedules in columns 1 and 2 in Activity 2.

★ One copy for each student of Activities 3, 4, and 5.
"Help Wanted" ads from local/regional/national publications brought in by students.

PROCEDURE

DAY ONE

1. Review the concepts of supply and demand as they apply to the labor force. (See Introduction.) Students' financial futures will be determined by their success in entering a labor market where there is a high demand for their services or products and a relatively small supply.

2. Explain that students are going to play a game to determine the wage rate in two separate markets; *do not* explain that one market is for unskilled workers and workers whose skills are not in high demand and one is for workers with those specific skills for which there is a high demand.

3. Divide class into two groups. Explain that one half will be prospective workers (sellers of labor) and one half will be prospective employers (buyers of labor). Each worker will try to get the highest wage possible, and each employer will try to pay the lowest wage possible. White cards will give the workers their directions and blue cards will give the employers their directions.

4. Each employer may hire as many workers as he or she is able to hire at the "correct" wage rate. Prospective employers should draw a card from the blue pile. Their cards will tell them how much they should pay for a worker. Their instructions will say, "You are looking for workers. Try to pay the lowest wage possible, and do not pay more than X per hour." Once a worker has been hired, the employer may return the card to the bottom of the blue pile, pick another card from the top of the pile and try to hire another worker.

5. Each worker (seller) will try to be hired as many times as possible, representing different workers in the market. Workers (sellers) should draw a card from the white pile. The instructions will say, "You are looking for work. Try to get the highest wage possible but do not take less than X per hour." Once a worker has been hired, he or she may return the card to the bottom of the white pile. The student should then represent another worker, pick another card from the top of the pile, and try for another job.

6. Appoint a monitor who will not play the game but will be sure that the directions are followed concerning cards being drawn from the top of the deck and replaced at the bottom of the deck. Appoint a recorder who will keep track of the wages at which workers are hired. The recorder should draw two columns on the left-hand side of a board. At the top of the two columns, the recorder should write "Labor Market 1." Column 1 should be entitled "Wage." The wages from column 1 of Activity 1 should be written down column 1 on the board. Column 2 should be "Total Number of Workers Hired at that Wage." (Prepare the board before class begins.)

7. When a worker has been hired, he or she should report the wage to the recorder. The recorder will put a check mark in column 2 next to the appropriate wage. Only the workers should report the wage. At the end of the activity, the recorder will sum up the number of check marks next to each wage to determine the total number of workers hired at each wage.

8. Tell students to begin. The game should last at least 10 minutes, or as long as it takes for wages to cluster around the equilibrium (somewhere around $4.30). At the end of the game have students take their seats. Have them look at the recorded wages and estimate the equilibrium wage (It should be around $4.30). Write "Equilibrium Wage = $4.30" (or whatever it turns out to be) next to the table on the left-hand side of the board.

9. On the right-hand side of the board have the recorder draw a table similar to the previous table, but this one should be labeled "Labor Market 2." The columns will be labeled exactly as the previous table. (Again, prepare the board before class begins.)

10. Repeat the game as before, using the pink and green cards that reflect the supply and demand conditions of Activity 2. At the end of the game have students take their seats. Have them

look at the recorded wages for workers hired and estimate the equilibrium wage. (It should be around $43.00.) Write "Equilibrium Wage = $43.00" (or whatever it turns out to be) next to the table on the right-hand side of the board.

11. Ask the students to compare the two labor markets. What types of workers do they think are involved in the two markets? Why are the wages in one market so much higher than in the other? Why did wages cluster around an equilibrium wage?

12. Distribute Activities 1 and 2. Have students graph the supply and demand for labor in both markets from the data on the sheets that correspond with the number of cards at each wage in the simulation. Explain that the sheets present the numbers that were used in the game they just played. Explain that students should use 20¢ increments for wages on the vertical axis and 2 worker increments on the horizontal axis for labor market 1. For labor market 2 they should use $2 increments on the vertical axis and 2 worker increments on the horizontal axis.

13. When students have completed the graphs, ask them to read the descriptions of the markets and the equilibrium wages from their graphs. Explain that Activity 1 corresponds to the left-hand side of the board and Activity 2 corresponds to the right-hand side of the board.

14. In labor market 1 explore why some people might work for $3.50 per hour and why some might not. (Answers could include opportunity cost; if a worker can earn more by collecting unemployment or welfare and might have to pay child care, transportation and clothing costs, a job at $3.50 per hour might not make economic sense. In addition, there is no security and few benefits. On the other hand, the job does provide a sense of responsibility and respect and could lead to something better.)
Since it is illegal in many jobs for employers to pay workers less than the minimum wage, why would some labor transactions take place at this wage?

This completes the exercise for Day 1.

DAY TWO

15. On Day 2, distribute Activity 3 (The SCANS Report). Discuss each of the eight skills, asking students to give an example of each one.

16. Once it is clear that students understand the skills, ask them to complete Activity 4, their Self-Appraisal. Select some students to explain one area in which they rated themselves as having good skills and one in which they rated themselves as needing improvement. Ask the class if they think these evaluations are realistic. For homework, have students complete as many Activity 5 forms (Plans for Self-Improvement) as appropriate.

This completes the exercise for Day 2.

DAY THREE

17. On Day 3, have selected students explain their plans to the class. Help them evaluate their plans based on the three criteria (short-term, measurable, and achievable). Be careful to evaluate the plans, not the students' abilities.

18. Have students evaluate their own plans based on the discussion from selected students and redo them as a result of the discussion.

19. Have students submit the plans to you and the guidance counselor, a parent, another adult or a friend. Depending on the number of students and the time allowed, either evaluate each student plan based on the three criteria , with suggestions for revision, or have them ask the "other person" to do so.

20. Have the students work with you or the "other person" to evaluate their plans. Periodically, have the students submit an update of the plans to you.

CLOSURE

On Day 4, have students bring in help wanted ads representative of both types of labor markets. Discuss the skills that are necessary for the higher paying jobs. Have students write an essay describing the nature of the job they would like to have, the skills needed for the job, and a summary of their plans to acquire the necessary skills.

ASSESSMENT

Grade the essay based on the realism and practicality of their plans to acquire skills. Are they considering all the skills they will need? Are they realistic in their plans for acquiring those skills?

THE CARDS

1. White: You are looking for work. Try to get the highest wage possible but do not take less than X per hour.

2. Blue: You are looking for workers. Try to pay the lowest wage possible and do not pay more than X per hour.

3. Pink: You are considering working in this industry. You are currently earning X per hour. Try to get the highest wage possible but do not accept less than your current wage.

4. Green: You wish to hire workers with specific skills. Try to pay the lowest wage possible, and do not pay more than X per hour.

THE BOARD

LABOR MARKET 1

Wage/Hour	Number of Workers Hired
$5.30	
5.20	
5.10	
5.00	
4.90	
4.80	
4.70	
4.60	
4.50	
4.40	
4.30	
4.20	
4.10	
4.00	
3.90	
3.80	
3.70	
3.60	
3.50	

LABOR MARKET 2

Wage/Hour	Number of Workers Hired
$53	
52	
51	
50	
49	
48	
47	
46	
45	
44	
43	
42	
41	
40	
39	
38	
37	
36	
35	

ACTIVITY 1

Name _____

Labor Market 1. Most of the jobs in this market are repetitive and monotonous. They require little skill . The jobs are not full-time and do not provide benefits. There is little chance for promotion or advancement. Most of the workers have a high school diploma or less. Some of the workers have highly technical skills that are no longer in demand.

Supply schedule: In this table, the second column is the number of workers who would be willing to work at the wage indicated in column 1. Recognize that they would, of course, be willing to work for a higher wage also. The third column is the cumulative number of workers that would be willing to work at the wage indicated or at a higher wage. For example, at a wage of $3.50, two workers would be willing to work. If the wage increases to $3.70, two more workers enter the market bringing to four the total number of workers willing to work at $3.70.

Wage	Additional number of workers willing and able to work at the wage indicated (White Cards)	Cumulative Supply Schedule (Total number of workers willing to work at this wage)
$5.10	4 workers	26
$4.90	4 workers	22
$4.70	4 workers	18
$4.50	4 workers	14
$4.30	2 workers	10
$4.10	2 workers	8
$3.90	2 workers	6
$3.70	2 workers	4
$3.50	2 workers	2

ACTIVITY 1 (CONTINUED)

Name _____

Demand schedule: In this table, the second column is the number of workers that employers would be willing to hire at the wage indicated in column 1. Recognize that the employer would, of course, be willing to hire this worker at a lower wage also. The third column is the cumulative number of workers that employers would be willing and able to hire at the wage indicated or at a lower price. For example, at a wage of $5.10, the employer who would hire at $5.30 would hire a worker at $5.10 and be very pleased that he or she did not have to pay $5.30; the employer who is willing and able to hire at $5.10 would also hire a worker. Two workers would be hired at $5.10. If the wage falls to $4.90, employers would be delighted that they don't have to pay $5.30 or $5.10 for the first two workers, and two more workers would be hired. The total number of workers hired at $4.90 would be 4 workers.

Wage	Additional number of workers that employers are willing and able to hire at the wage indicated (Blue Cards)	Demand Schedule (Total number of workers employers would hire at this wage)
$5.30	1 worker	1
$5.10	1 worker	2
$4.90	2 workers	4
$4.70	2 workers	6
$4.50	2 workers	8
$4.30	2 workers	10
$4.10	2 workers	12
$3.90	2 workers	14
$3.70	4 workers	18
$3.50	4 workers	22

ACTIVITY 2

Name _____

This is the market for workers in a specific high skilled industry. The job is interesting and rewarding and the sky is the limit in terms of advancement. The work is high pressure with tight deadlines. Many people in this industry work long hours and weekends. The job is not for everyone. All of the workers in this industry have technical skills or college degrees, many have masters degrees and some have Ph.Ds. The job requires a great deal of skill, analytical ability, and common sense.

Supply schedule: In this table, the supply schedule in the third column is the cumulative number of workers available for hire at the wage indicated or at a higher wage.

Wage	Additional number of workers willing and able to work at the wage indicated (Pink Cards)	Supply Schedule (Total number of workers willing to work at this wage)
$51	4 workers	22
$49	4 workers	18
$47	4 workers	14
$45	2 workers	10
$43	2 workers	8
$41	2 workers	6
$39	2 workers	4
$37	1 worker	2
$35	1 worker	1

From *Personal Decision Making: Focus on Economics,* © National Council on Economic Education, New York, NY

ACTIVITY 2 (CONTINUED)

Name _____

Demand schedule: In this table, the demand schedule in the third column is the cumulative number of workers employers would be willing and able to hire at the wage indicated or at a lower price.

Wage	Additional number of workers that employers are willing and able to hire at the wage indicated (Green Cards)	Demand Schedule (Total number of workers employers would hire at this wage)
$51	2 workers	2
$49	2 workers	4
$47	2 workers	6
$45	2 workers	8
$43	2 workers	10
$41	2 workers	12
$39	4 workers	16
$37	4 workers	20
$35	4 workers	24
$33	4 workers	28

WORKER CARDS FOR ACTIVITY 1

(Make 2 copies of this sheet)

 WORKER
Labor Market 1

You are looking for work. Try to get the highest wage possible, but do not take less than $5.10 per hour.

 WORKER
Labor Market 1

You are looking for work. Try to get the highest wage possible, but do not take less than $5.10 per hour.

 WORKER
Labor Market 1

You are looking for work. Try to get the highest wage possible, but do not take less than $4.90 per hour.

 WORKER
Labor Market 1

You are looking for work. Try to get the highest wage possible, but do not take less than $4.90 per hour.

 WORKER
Labor Market 1

You are looking for work. Try to get the highest wage possible, but do not take less than $4.70 per hour.

 WORKER
Labor Market 1

You are looking for work. Try to get the highest wage possible, but do not take less than $4.70 per hour.

 WORKER
Labor Market 1

You are looking for work. Try to get the highest wage possible, but do not take less than $4.50 per hour.

 WORKER
Labor Market 1

You are looking for work. Try to get the highest wage possible, but do not take less than $4.50 per hour.

 WORKER
Labor Market 1

You are looking for work. Try to get the highest wage possible, but do not take less than $4.30 per hour.

 WORKER
Labor Market 1

You are looking for work. Try to get the highest wage possible, but do not take less than $4.10 per hour.

 WORKER
Labor Market 1

You are looking for work. Try to get the highest wage possible, but do not take less than $3.90 per hour.

WORKER
Labor Market 1

You are looking for work. Try to get the highest wage possible, but do not take less than $3.70 per hour.

WORKER
Labor Market 1

You are looking for work. Try to get the highest wage possible, but do not take less than $3.50 per hour.

EMPLOYER CARDS FOR ACTIVITY 1

(Make only 1 copy of this sheet)

EMPLOYER
Labor Market 1

You want to hire skilled workers. Try to pay the lowest wage possible, but do not pay more than $5.30 per hour.

EMPLOYER
Labor Market 1

You want to hire skilled workers. Try to pay the lowest wage possible, but do not pay more than $5.10 per hour.

EMPLOYER
Labor Market 1

You want to hire skilled workers. Try to pay the lowest wage possible, but do not pay more than $4.90 per hour.

EMPLOYER
Labor Market 1

You want to hire skilled workers. Try to pay the lowest wage possible, but do not pay more than $4.90 per hour.

EMPLOYER
Labor Market 1

You want to hire skilled workers. Try to pay the lowest wage possible, but do not pay more than $4.70 per hour.

EMPLOYER
Labor Market 1

You want to hire skilled workers. Try to pay the lowest wage possible, but do not pay more than $4.70 per hour.

EMPLOYER
Labor Market 1

You want to hire skilled workers. Try to pay the lowest wage possible, but do not pay more than $4.50 per hour.

EMPLOYER
Labor Market 1

You want to hire skilled workers. Try to pay the lowest wage possible, but do not pay more than $4.50 per hour.

EMPLOYER
Labor Market 1

You want to hire skilled workers. Try to pay the lowest wage possible, but do not pay more than $4.30 per hour.

EMPLOYER
Labor Market 1

You want to hire skilled workers. Try to pay the lowest wage possible, but do not pay more than $4.30 per hour.

EMPLOYER
Labor Market 1

You want to hire skilled workers. Try to pay the lowest wage possible, but do not pay more than $4.10 per hour.

EMPLOYER
Labor Market 1

You want to hire skilled workers. Try to pay the lowest wage possible, but do not pay more than $4.10 per hour.

EMPLOYER
Labor Market 1

You want to hire skilled workers. Try to pay the lowest wage possible, but do not pay more than $3.90 per hour.

EMPLOYER
Labor Market 1

You want to hire skilled workers. Try to pay the lowest wage possible, but do not pay more than $3.90 per hour.

EMPLOYER CARDS FOR ACTIVITY 1

(Make only 1 copy of this sheet)

 EMPLOYER
Labor Market 1

You want to hire skilled workers. Try to pay the lowest wage possible, but do not pay more than $3.70 per hour.

 EMPLOYER
Labor Market 1

You want to hire skilled workers. Try to pay the lowest wage possible, but do not pay more than $3.70 per hour.

 EMPLOYER
Labor Market 1

You want to hire skilled workers. Try to pay the lowest wage possible, but do not pay more than $3.70 per hour.

 EMPLOYER
Labor Market 1

You want to hire skilled workers. Try to pay the lowest wage possible, but do not pay more than $3.70 per hour.

EMPLOYER
Labor Market 1

You want to hire skilled workers. Try to pay the lowest wage possible, but do not pay more than $3.50 per hour.

 EMPLOYER
Labor Market 1

You want to hire skilled workers. Try to pay the lowest wage possible, but do not pay more than $3.50 per hour.

 EMPLOYER
Labor Market 1

You want to hire skilled workers. Try to pay the lowest wage possible, but do not pay more than $3.50 per hour.

 EMPLOYER
Labor Market 1

You want to hire skilled workers. Try to pay the lowest wage possible, but do not pay more than $3.50 per hour.

WORKER CARDS FOR ACTIVITY 2

(Make 2 copies of these cards)

WORKER
Labor Market 2
You are considering working in this industry. You are currently employed and earning $51 per hour. Try to get the highest wage possible, but do not accept less than your current wage.

WORKER
Labor Market 2
You are considering working in this industry. You are currently employed and earning $51 per hour. Try to get the highest wage possible, but do not accept less than your current wage.

WORKER
Labor Market 2
You are considering working in this industry. You are currently employed and earning $49 per hour. Try to get the highest wage possible, but do not accept less than your current wage.

WORKER
Labor Market 2
You are considering working in this industry. You are currently employed and earning $49 per hour. Try to get the highest wage possible, but do not accept less than your current wage.

WORKER
Labor Market 2
You are considering working in this industry. You are currently employed and earning $47 per hour. Try to get the highest wage possible, but do not accept less than your current wage.

WORKER
Labor Market 2
You are considering working in this industry. You are currently employed and earning $47 per hour. Try to get the highest wage possible, but do not accept less than your current wage.

WORKER
Labor Market 2
You are considering working in this industry. You are currently employed and earning $45 per hour. Try to get the highest wage possible, but do not accept less than your current wage.

WORKER
Labor Market 2
You are considering working in this industry. You are currently employed and earning $43 per hour. Try to get the highest wage possible, but do not accept less than your current wage.

WORKER
Labor Market 2
You are considering working in this industry. You are currently employed and earning $41 per hour. Try to get the highest wage possible, but do not accept less than your current wage.

WORKER
Labor Market 2
You are considering working in this industry. You are currently employed and earning $39 per hour. Try to get the highest wage possible, but do not accept less than your current wage.

Make only one copy of these cards.

WORKER
Labor Market 2
You are considering working in this industry. You are currently employed and earning $37 per hour. Try to get the highest wage possible, but do not accept less than your current wage.

WORKER
Labor Market 2
You are considering working in this industry. You are currently employed and earning $35 per hour. Try to get the highest wage possible, but do not accept less than your current wage.

EMPLOYER CARDS FOR ACTIVITY 2

(Make only 1 copy of this sheet)

EMPLOYER
Labor Market 2

You want to hire skilled workers. Try to pay the lowest wage possible, but do not pay more than $51 per hour.

EMPLOYER
Labor Market 2

You want to hire skilled workers. Try to pay the lowest wage possible, but do not pay more than $51 per hour.

EMPLOYER
Labor Market 2

You want to hire skilled workers. Try to pay the lowest wage possible, but do not pay more than $49 per hour.

EMPLOYER
Labor Market 2

You want to hire skilled workers. Try to pay the lowest wage possible, but do not pay more than $49 per hour.

EMPLOYER
Labor Market 2

You want to hire skilled workers. Try to pay the lowest wage possible, but do not pay more than $47 per hour.

EMPLOYER
Labor Market 2

You want to hire skilled workers. Try to pay the lowest wage possible, but do not pay more than $47 per hour.

EMPLOYER
Labor Market 2

You want to hire skilled workers. Try to pay the lowest wage possible, but do not pay more than $45 per hour.

EMPLOYER
Labor Market 2

You want to hire skilled workers. Try to pay the lowest wage possible, but do not pay more than $45 per hour.

EMPLOYER
Labor Market 2

You want to hire skilled workers. Try to pay the lowest wage possible, but do not pay more than $43 per hour.

EMPLOYER
Labor Market 2

You want to hire skilled workers. Try to pay the lowest wage possible, but do not pay more than $43 per hour.

EMPLOYER
Labor Market 2

You want to hire skilled workers. Try to pay the lowest wage possible, but do not pay more than $41 per hour.

EMPLOYER
Labor Market 2

You want to hire skilled workers. Try to pay the lowest wage possible, but do not pay more than $41 per hour.

EMPLOYER CARDS FOR ACTIVITY 2

(Make 2 copies of this sheet)

 EMPLOYER
Labor Market 2

You want to hire skilled workers. Try to pay the lowest wage possible, but do not pay more than $39 per hour.

 EMPLOYER
Labor Market 2

You want to hire skilled workers. Try to pay the lowest wage possible, but do not pay more than $39 per hour.

 **EMPLOYER**
Labor Market 2

You want to hire skilled workers. Try to pay the lowest wage possible, but do not pay more than $37 per hour.

 EMPLOYER
Labor Market 2

You want to hire skilled workers. Try to pay the lowest wage possible, but do not pay more than $37 per hour.

 EMPLOYER
Labor Market 2

You want to hire skilled workers. Try to pay the lowest wage possible, but do not pay more than $35 per hour.

 EMPLOYER
Labor Market 2

You want to hire skilled workers. Try to pay the lowest wage possible, but do not pay more than $35 per hour.

 EMPLOYER
Labor Market 2

You want to hire skilled workers. Try to pay the lowest wage possible, but do not pay more than $33 per hour.

 EMPLOYER
Labor Market 2

You want to hire skilled workers. Try to pay the lowest wage possible, but do not pay more than $33 per hour.

ACTIVITY 3
THE SCANS REPORT

Name _____

The Secretary's Commission on Achieving Necessary Skills (SCANS), produced by the U.S. Secretary of Labor in 1990, describes the skills that are necessary for all jobs in the workplace.

Basic Skills: Minimum skills necessary for anyone who wishes to hold even a low skilled job. They include reading, writing, arithmetic and mathematics, listening, and speaking.

Thinking Skills: Skills that allow workers to analyze situations, and include creative thinking, decision making, problem solving, visualizing, knowing how to learn, and reasoning.

Personal Qualities: Perhaps more important than the skills the worker brings to the job are his or her personal characteristics. Employers are as concerned with "Who you are," as they are with "What you can do." Characteristics important to the workplace are individual responsibility, self-esteem, sociability, self-management, and integrity.

Resources: People allocate resources in many daily activities, such as developing a monthly household budget or scheduling the diverse activities of family members. Allocating resources—labor, materials, income—is equally important on the job. The task includes planning, organizing, monitoring, assessing, evaluating, and adjusting.

Interpersonal Skills: The skills in this category are becoming increasingly important as teamwork becomes more common in the workplace. The skills in this category include participating as a member of a team, teaching others, serving clients/customers, exercising leadership, negotiating to arrive at a decision, and working with people from culturally diverse backgrounds.

Systems: Effective workers understand social, organizational, and technological systems. They monitor and correct performance, and they monitor and correct systems. They can answer such questions as, "How is it supposed to work, how does it work, how can we improve it?"

Information: Workers of today find, use, evaluate, and communicate information. The skills included in this category are acquiring and evaluating, organizing and maintaining, interpreting and communicating, and using computers to process information.

Technology: Effective workers select equipment and tools, they apply technology to specific tasks, and they maintain and trouble shoot technologies. Given current and future technological advances, workers must be up-to-date on the latest technology, and willing to learn new ones.

The following two pages help you evaluate your current skills and develop plans for improvement in those areas where improvement is needed.

ACTIVITY 4
SCANS SELF-APPRAISAL

Name _____

1. **Basic skills:** reading, writing, arithmetic and mathematics, speaking, and listening.

    Good skills _____   OK _____   Need help _____

2. **Thinking skills:** Thinking creatively, making decisions, solving problems, seeing things in the mind's eye, knowing how to learn, reasoning.

    Good skills _____   OK _____   Need help _____

3. **Personal qualities:** individual responsibility, self-esteem, sociability, self-management, and integrity.

    Good skills _____   OK _____   Need help _____

4. **Resources:** Allocating time, money, materials, space, and staff.

    Good skills _____   OK _____   Need help _____

5. **Interpersonal skills:** working on teams, teaching others, serving customers, leading negotiating, and working well with people from culturally diverse backgrounds.

    Good skills _____   OK _____   Need help _____

6. **Information:** Acquiring and evaluating data, organizing and maintaining files, interpreting and communicating, and using computers to process information.

    Good skills _____   OK _____   Need help _____

7. **Systems:** understanding social, organizational, and technological systems, monitoring and correcting performance, and designing or improving systems.

    Good skills _____   OK _____   Need help _____

8. **Technology:** selecting equipment and tools, applying technology to specific tasks, and maintaining and troubleshooting equipment.

    Good skills _____   OK _____   Need help _____

ACTIVITY 5
PLAN FOR SELF-IMPROVEMENT

Name_____

Use this sheet to set particular goals and activities to help improve particular skills from the list on the previous page. Goals should be short term, measurable, and achievable, such as "Improve my math grade by a letter grade on the next report card. " One activity could be "Make sure that I successfully complete and understand my math homework." Find someone (teacher, parent, friend) who will help you monitor your progress with the goals. Once you feel comfortable that you have reached your goals, set new and higher ones.

In order to become more productive, I plan to improve the following skills.

_____   _____   _____

The following goals and activities will help me improve these skills.

1. Skill _____   Goal _____

   Activities to achieve my goal

   _____
   _____

   Start date_____   Completion date_____

2. Skill _____   Goal _____

   Activities to achieve my goal

   _____
   _____

   Start date_____   Completion date_____

3. Skill _____   Goal _____

   Activities to achieve my goal

   _____
   _____

   Start date_____   Completion date_____

LESSON 5
PRICE AS A RATIONING METHOD: HOW DOES A MARKET WORK?

INTRODUCTION

What is the function of a price? Why is the price of a diamond, which has little practical value, higher than the price of a life-saving drug such as insulin? In a market economy, scarce goods and services are allocated through the price mechanism. A higher price reflects the fact that a good or service is relatively more scarce than a lower priced good or service. It is important to note that this is not primarily a lesson on specific price determination. Most students do not recognize the reason why a market economy has prices and they do not make the link between relative scarcity and relative prices; the specific price is determined by specific supply and demand data. This lesson explains the reason for prices and the general relationship between changes in supply and demand that will cause a price to increase or decrease.

CONCEPTS

Scarcity
Allocation
Relative price
More scarce
Less scarce

CONTENT STANDARD

Scarcity is the condition of not being able to have all of the goods and services that one wants.

Relative prices refer to the price of one good or service compared to the prices of other goods and services, and are the basic measure of the relative scarcity of a product when prices are set by market forces (supply and demand).

OBJECTIVES

◆ Recognize price as the major allocative mechanism in a market economy.

◆ List the ways in which a good can become more scarce.

◆ Identify the direction of the price change if a good becomes more scarce.

◆ List the ways in which a good can become less scarce.

◆ Identify the direction of the price change if a good becomes less scarce.

LESSON DESCRIPTION

Students use the price mechanism to allocate scarce goods and one good which may not be scarce.

TIME REQUIRED

Two class periods.

MATERIALS

Eleven relatively inexpensive items such as pencils, apples, small snacks, or key chains and one item that is even less expensive such as a bottle cap.
★ Copies of Activities 1 and 2 for each student. Visuals 1, 2, 3, 4, 5, and 6.

PROCEDURE

DAY ONE

1. Ask students to help you solve a mystery. Why don't grocers simply give food away when some people can't afford to pay for food? The eventual answer should reflect the fact that the production of food involves the use of scarce resources that have an opportunity cost.

2. Ask students why those of them who work for wages don't simply give their labor away? Once again, the answer should reflect the fact that their labor is scarce and allocating it to working involves an opportunity cost for which they must be compensated.

The point is that people charge for goods and services that are scarce. Explain that a good is scarce if allocating it involves an opportunity cost. A free good or service is one that has no opportunity cost. If it has an opportunity cost, then the price reflects that opportunity cost. On the supply side, prices reflect the opportunity costs of scarce resources used to produce a product.

3. Ask students why grocers don't charge $5000 for a carrot? Why don't those who work for wages charge $10,000 per hour? Answers should reflect the fact that sellers are disciplined by the laws of the market. All products face a demand curve and sellers are not likely to find buyers who would want carrots at $5000 a piece, and workers are not likely to find many employers who are willing to pay $10,000 per hour.

Summarize by explaining that sellers hope to recoup the opportunity costs of scarce resources used in production and buyers will pay only what the product is worth to them. These two considerations, opportunity costs of production and value to buyers, determine the price of a scarce product. Emphasize that relative scarcity is the relationship between the supply of a product and the demand for the product.

4. Show students a product (an inexpensive item such as an apple or something else that students are likely to want and be willing to pay for). Explain that there is only one of these items and that you are going to allocate the product using the price mechanism. Auction the product and take the highest price, after everyone else has been bid out of the market. Be sure to collect the money and keep a record of the price.

5. Ask students why you didn't simply give the item to everyone. The answer is that you only had one and the class contains more than one student who wanted the item and was willing and able to pay for it. The good was scarce. Scarcity means that there isn't enough to go around; the amount of the product available is not sufficient to satisfy everyone's wants for the product. The scarce good had to be allocated. When a scarce good is allocated, some are told, "Yes," and others are told, "No."

6. When a product is scarce, a method of allocation must be used. Ask students what method you used in Step 4 to allocate the scarce good. *Answer:* price method. Now ask the students what the function of price is in a market economy? *Answer:* the function of price in a market economy

is the allocation of scarce resources and goods and services.

7. Did the price seem relatively high or low? Hopefully, students will say that the price was high. Why? The amount available was very low (one) relative to the wants of the class.

DAY TWO

8. Bring in ten of the same items. Let students know that you have ten and that you are going to auction them. Sell them, one by one, until all are gone. Collect the money and keep a record of the prices. Ask students if the average price today is higher or lower than yesterday. Why? Demand probably did not change, but the amount available was greater today than yesterday. Supply is higher relative to demand, the good is relatively less scarce than yesterday. The price of one product relative to another reflects the relative scarcity of the item.

DAY THREE

9. Let students know that you have an item that people are not likely to be willing to pay for such as a bottle cap or a rubber band. Attempt to auction the item. If someone buys it for a low price, that is fine; if they don't, that is fine also.

10. Review the experience of Day 1. Ask students why the price was so high. The answer should be that there was a great deal of demand, and little supply; the good was relatively scarce. Why was the price of the same item lower on Day 2? The supply was greater relative to demand, so the good was less scarce. Why was the price of the third item so low or zero? Either the good was not scarce or was relatively less scarce than the other items. Even though the supply was low, demand was either zero or very low.

CLOSURE

11. Two lessons come from this activity:

A. Scarce goods must be allocated and a market economy uses the price system to perform this allocative function. The market method is one way to determine who gets the products people offer for sale.

B. The price of one product relative to another reflects the relative scarcity of that item offered in the market by suppliers (producers) of the product or service compared to how much demanders (consumers) are willing and able to buy. Although diamonds may have little practical use, the supply is low relative to demand and diamond prices are high. Wealthy people who want diamonds can get them in the market, those who want diamonds but have no resources to buy them, cannot. Although water is essential to life and billions of people need it, fortunately the supply of water is still relatively high compared to the amount people demand and the relatively low price per gallon permits most people to buy what they want. Prices reflect relative scarcity, determined by the relationship between supply and demand.

12. Use Visuals 1 to 6 to illustrate that prices allocate scarce goods and services in a market economy. (These can be used as transparency masters.)

> A good becomes more scarce if one of two things happens:
>   a. the supply decreases, or
>   b. the demand increases.
> If a good becomes more scarce, the price will rise.

> A good becomes less scarce if one of two things happens:
>   a. the supply increases, or
>   b. the demand decreases.
> If a good becomes less scarce, the price will fall.

The important point is that neither demand nor supply alone determines the price of a product. A decrease in supply will not raise the price if demand decreases by the same amount. The relative scarcity of a product is determined by the relationship between supply and demand.

ASSESSMENT

Divide the class into groups of four. Distribute Activity 1 and Activity 2. Have each group complete both activities and be prepared to defend their answers. Discuss the correct responses to the exercises.

> *Answer:* 2, 3, 4, 6, 8, and 10 are scarce.
> The relative scarcity of the items are as follows: 6, 10, 3, 8, 2, 4
> The indicator of relative scarcity is the price of the item.

ACTIVITY 1

Name _____

Identify each of the following as scarce (S) or not scarce (N). Rank these items that are scarce in order of relative scarcity from most scarce (1) to least scarce. Explain what you used as an indicator of relative scarcity.

Item	Scarce or Not Scarce?	If Scarce, Rank
1. Garbage		
2. A gallon of purified water		
3. A compact disk		
4. A pencil		
5. Air		
6. A sports car		
7. Annoying noise		
8. A ticket to a movie		
9. Traffic congestion		
10. A pair of high quality shoes		

ACTIVITY 2

Name_____

Identify whether the following events will cause the product to become relatively more (M) or less (L) scarce, and whether the price will rise (R) or fall (F) as a result.

Market	More or Less Scarce	Price Rise or Fall
1. Coffee		
2. Cola		
3. U2 concert		
4. Gasoline		
5. Water		
6. Cellular phone		
7. Computer		
8. Nurse		
9. Small truck		
10. Audiotape		

1. A frost wipes out the coffee crop in the two major coffee producing countries, Brazil and Colombia.

2. Most cola drinkers become convinced that cola is bad for their health, causing cancer and heart disease.

3. The rock group U2 clones itself, so that there are now 100 U2 groups performing around the world.

4. Summer arrives and people decide to drive long distances for vacation.

5. A drought causes the water supply to drop to 50% of its normal level.

6. People become convinced that cellular phones are protection against roadside crime.

7. Many new computer producers begin production, lured by high profits in the industry.

8. The product is a nurse. Many people decide not to enter the nursing profession as many older nurses retire.

9. Many people decide small trucks are their vehicle of choice.

10. Some people decide that compact disks, not tapes, are the way to listen to music.

11. In general, what can you say about the price of a good or service when it becomes more scarce? less scarce?

ACTIVITY 2 ANSWERS

Market	More or Less Scarce	Price Rise or Fall
1. Coffee	M	R
2. Cola	L	F
3. U2 concert	L	F
4. Gasoline	M	R
5. Water	M	R
6. Cellular phone	M	R
7. Computer	L	F
8. Nurse	M	R
9. Small truck	M	R
10. Audiotape	L	F

11. When a good or service becomes more scarce, the price rises; when it becomes less scarce, the price falls.

VISUAL 1
LOW DEMAND, LOW SUPPLY

VISUAL 2
HIGH DEMAND, HIGH SUPPLY

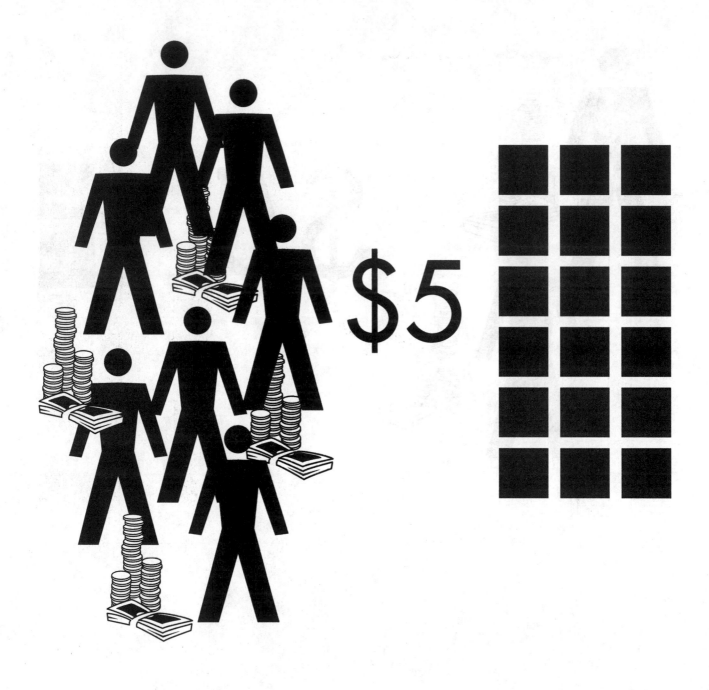

VISUAL 3
LOW DEMAND, HIGH SUPPLY

Sellers ask, "How can we get rid of this stuff? It is less scarce than it used to be,"
Answer: "Lower the price."

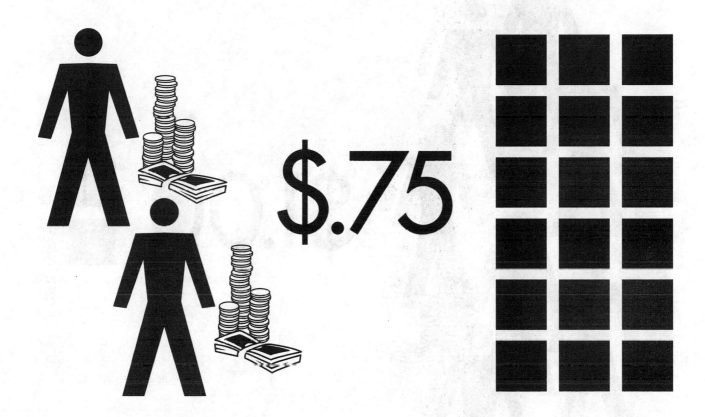

VISUAL 4
HIGH DEMAND, LOW SUPPLY

Many buyers bid against each other for goods that are now more scarce, driving the price up.

$1.00 ▬

 From *Personal Decision Making: Focus on Economics,* © National Council on Economic Education, New York, NY

VISUAL 5
A GOOD OR SERVICE BECOMES MORE SCARCE IF:

1. Supply decreases, or

2. Demand increases.

If a good or service becomes more scarce, price will increase.

VISUAL 6
A GOOD OR SERVICE BECOMES LESS SCARCE IF:

1. Supply increases, or

2. Demand decreases.

If a good or service becomes less scarce, price will decrease.

 From *Personal Decision Making: Focus on Economics,* © National Council on Economic Education, New York, NY

LESSON 6
FINANCIAL PLANNING: BUDGETING YOUR FINANCIAL RESOURCES

INTRODUCTION

Financial planning is a reasoned approach to allocating economic resources to maximize the satisfaction one gets from life. A financial plan or budget is a convenient decision-making tool which is based on the fundamental economic principles of scarcity, choice, and opportunity cost. In the absence of a financial plan, impulse buying may make it difficult to "make ends meet" no matter the level of income. It is important to realize that every purchase involves cost—opportunity cost. Maximizing satisfaction depends on an analysis of the costs and benefits of purchases. Equipped with an understanding of the financial planning process, students are better able to adapt to ever-changing economic conditions.

CONCEPTS
Scarcity
Opportunity cost
Income
Purchasing power
Fixed expenses
Variable expenses
Impulse buying

CONTENT STANDARD
Scarcity requires people to make choices about using goods and services to satisfy wants.

OBJECTIVES
◆ Identify the opportunity cost of a decision to purchase a good or service.

◆ Explain that income is the result of productive activities in the economy.

◆ Identify sources of income.

◆ Identify living expenses.

◆ Distinguish between fixed and variable expenses.

◆ Develop a personal budget.

◆ Compare and contrast several budgets for individuals upon leaving school.

LESSON DESCRIPTION
Students participate in a motivational activity in which they evaluate the costs and benefits of impulse buying and its effect on living on a limited income. After they analyze a sample budget, students develop their own budget that might be appropriate upon leaving school.

TIME REQUIRED
Two or three class periods.

MATERIALS
Pictures of approximately 20–25 items, which may be laminated. The items should be divided into the following broad budget categories:
Housing (an apartment and/or house, which represents living with parents)
Utilities (electric, gas, oil, telephone, etc.)
Installment payments (car, credit card payments, etc.)
Insurance (auto, home owner, etc.)
Savings (bank, club payments, etc.)
Transportation (gas, oil, etc.)
Food (at home)
Eating out (restaurants, picnics, etc.)
Clothing (both moderate and high-priced clothing)
Personal care (shampoo, etc.)
Household (supplies and furnishings)
Recreation and entertainment (movies, concerts, etc.)
Miscellaneous items (include a large number of favorite items that students might tend to buy on impulse and a card representing a realistic income tax rate)

Label each picture with a realistic price. Randomly assemble the pictures, but sprinkle more of the very popular, impulse items toward the beginning of the order.

★ Two copies for each student of Activity 1.
★ One copy for each student of Activity 2.
★ One copy for each student of Activity 3.
  Newspapers and catalogs

PROCEDURE

IMPULSE BUYING

1. Explain that the purpose of this lesson is to examine the effectiveness of making planned purchasing decisions and to apply this process to personal situations. Tell them that through their productive efforts they have $768 per month net income (approximately 40 hours/week @ $6/hour, 4 weeks per month, less payroll and Social Security taxes @ 20%). They are to use this income to buy those things that they might want if they were living independently. Brainstorm some items students think they would want to purchase (food, clothing, shelter, personal care, transportation, entertainment, etc.) *Note:* You may choose a monthly wage appropriate for your specific group of students.

2. Explain that you have assembled a variety of items you believe they may want to buy in order to live independently after finishing school. They must follow a few simple rules when making their purchases. Distribute Activity 1.

A. Give students thorough instructions for completing the form:

- Place the amount of money that they have to spend on the first line of the "Balance" column. ($768 initially)
- Enter the name of the item they choose to purchase in the "Item" column.
- The quantity of the item purchased is entered in the column labeled "Quantity."
- The price of the item is entered in the "Price" column.
- The "Total" column is an extension of the quantity times price.
- Each purchase is subtracted from the previous balance much like a checkbook.

B. The students may purchase as many items as they desire, but they may not spend more than their monthly income.

C. Once an item has been shown, no changes may be made. Students may not reverse a decision to buy any item, change the quantity, or purchase items previously displayed.

3. Display the items and corresponding prices one at a time according to the instructions in "C" above.

4. After all items have been shown, ask the class the following questions:

A. Who would be able to live independently with the items you chose to purchase? (Some students may find that because they spent some of their money on impulse items they would be unable to live independently. They might have had unrealistic ideas about the costs involved.)

B. Ask: Why were you unable to purchase all the items you wanted? (Not enough money.) Why did you run out of money? (Ask a few volunteers to share their list of purchases. These students, and others, probably bought a few impulse items.) Explain to the students that they exhibited impulse buying behavior.

5. Explain that decisions are not costless. *Scarcity* requires people to make choices about using goods and services to satisfy wants. Scarcity results from the imbalance between relatively unlimited wants and limited resources. For every choice there is an opportunity cost. *Opportunity cost* is the highest valued alternative that must be forgone because another option is chosen. (You might want to spend more time discussing and giving examples of scarcity and opportunity cost.) Ask:

A. What was the last item you purchased? (answers will vary.)

B. Is there another item you wanted to purchase but could not? (answers will vary.)

C. Emphasize that opportunity cost is the

value of the next best alternative forgone. Ask students to state their choice and identify their opportunity cost: "The opportunity cost of purchasing [the last item purchased] is [the item they did not purchase]."

6. Have the class suggest things that would help them make more informed decisions and achieve greater satisfaction from their limited income. (information on what items are in the market basket and their corresponding prices, information on substitute goods and services, a spending plan or budget.)

7. Tell the students that you will return to this shopping trip after they have learned how to manage their money.

FINANCIAL PLANNING

1. Explain that a budget is a planning tool that can be used to help individuals and families manage their money. The budget can be used to maximize their consumption potential and standard of living.

2. Distribute Activity 2. Use this sample budget as the basis for the following discussion on how to make a budget. (*Note:* This sample is an actual budget for a college student who is not dependent on parents. You may want to modify the budget to reflect your students' situations.) They will use the following steps in the budget process:

A. The first step is to identify sources of income. What are the sources of income in this budget? List the sources of income on the chalkboard. Ask students to think of other sources, and add these to the list. (gifts, dividends, tips, commissions) Add all income entries, and enter the total at the end of Step 1 ($975).

B. Next, identify living expenses. Tell students it is helpful to keep a log of monthly expenses to determine spending habits. There are two types of expenses. Those that remain the same each month are *fixed expenses*. Examples of fixed expenses

include rent, car payments, insurance, a monthly savings plan, etc. Expenses that change each month are called *variable expenses*. Examples of variable expenses include clothing, food, entertainment, personal allowances, etc. Have the students locate the fixed and variable expenses in the sample budget. List the fixed expenses in one column on the board and the variable expenses in another column. Ask students to offer other examples of things they might wish to buy that do not appear on the list. Have them classify the expense as either fixed or variable and add to the appropriate column on the board. (Fixed expenses: other installment debt, life and health insurance, etc. Variable expenses: charity, medical care, vacations, etc.)

Refer to the sample budget. Ask students to compute all fixed expenses and enter the amount under Step 2 on the worksheet ($620). Do the same for all variable expenses under Step 3 ($355). Finally, compute the total expenses by adding the fixed and variable expense totals. Enter this total on the worksheet ($975).

C. What's the bottom line? Compare expenses and income. Subtract the total expenses from income. Enter this amount in Step 4 ($0). The cash balance should be zero; that is, income and expenses should equal. If the cash balance is greater than zero, income is greater than living expenses. Ask students to suggest what someone might do with this money. (Save extra for a special purchase or an emergency, reevaluate and revise expense items, etc.) If the answer is less than zero, then projected expenses are greater than projected income. Ask students to suggest adjustments that might be made to balance the budget. (Reduce expenses, reduce unnecessary spending, increase income.)

MAKING IT ON YOUR OWN

1. Explain that they will now work in small groups to develop their own sample budget follow-

ing the format given in Activity 2.

2. Divide students into groups of three or four. Distribute Activity 3 to each student and provide each group with some newspapers and catalogs. These materials will help students calculate how much they might spend in each category. Remind them that these are estimates. Their income should be equal to the amount given in Step 1 of the Impulse Buying Game ($750 in this example).

3. Each student will develop his or her own budget by completing Activity 3. Students may share information with their group members.

4. Have students present their budgets to the class. This exercise will emphasize the point that all budgets are personal and unique to the individual. There is no definitive budget. Students will have an opportunity to discuss realistic income and expenses for different life situations.

5. Allow students time to adjust their budgets after this discussion.

CLOSURE

1. Once students have completed their budgets, distribute another copy of Activity 1. Tell them that you will repeat the shopping trip. The students will begin with their original monthly income. They are to use this income to buy those things that they must have to live independently. The budget they prepared for themselves in Activity 3 should be a guideline.

2. Tell the students that the same rules apply, but there is an additional rule. They must make purchases in the following budget categories:

> Housing
> Utilities
> Food
> Clothing
> Transportation
> Insurance
> All other purchases are discretionary.

Tell the students that the government must collect 15% for income tax. Deduct this from the account.

3. Show the items in the same order and allow students time to make their choices. After all items have been shown a second time, ask the class the following questions:

A. Did you purchase different items during the second shopping trip? What were some of the changes you made? (answers will vary.)

B. Why were you able to make these new purchases? (there was more information about choices and prices of possible items)

C. Are you more satisfied with your standard of living after the second shopping trip? How did the budget help you spend money more effectively? (able to make substitutes, didn't spend money on entertainment or luxury items at the expense of basic necessities)

EXTENSION

1. A writing portfolio project might include an essay comparing and contrasting their purchasing decisions in the two shopping trips. There should be some discussion on the opportunity cost of choices.

2. Ask students to select a career that they would like to pursue. Have them research the average starting salary for that career. Redistribute Activity 3 to the students and have them develop their own budget based on the salary information they gathered.

ACTIVITY 1
SHOPPING LIST

Name_____

Item	Quantity	Price	Total	Balance
Beginning Balance				$

ACTIVITY 2
SAMPLE BUDGET

Name _____

Michelle, 20 years old, is a full-time student at a regional four-year college. She lives in an apartment close to campus with a roommate who pays half of the rent and utilities. Michelle works 25 hours in a secretarial position at the college and 15 hours at a local department store as a sales clerk. The college provides medical coverage at no cost for each single employee (family plans require additional payment by the employee). Complete the following monthly budget.

Step 1: List Income
Salary (after taxes/deductions)	$	970
Interest (from savings)		5
Total Take Home Pay	$	____

Step 2: List Fixed Expenses
Housing (rent or mortgage)	$	170
Utilities (electricity, heating, water)		30
Telephone (basic service)		10
Installment payments (car)		100
Insurance (car)		90
Tuition		150
Savings (put in bank each month)		70
Total Fixed Expenses	$	____

Step 3: List Variable Expenses
Clothing and personal care	$	50
Food (at home and meals out)		110
Household supplies		20
College Expenses		45
Entertainment		35
Transportation (gas,oil,etc.)		50
Personal Allowances		20
Other (toll calls, etc.)		25
Total Variable Expenses	$	____
Total All Expenses	$	____

Step 4: Comparison
Total Cash Available (from Step 1)	$	____
Less Total Expenses (from Step 3)	$	____
Cash Balance	$	____

ACTIVITY 3
MAKING IT ON YOUR OWN

Name _____

Step 1: List Income
    Salary (after taxes/deductions)
    Interest (from savings)

    Total Take Home Pay

Step 2: List Fixed Expenses
    Housing (rent or mortgage)
    Utilities (electricity, heating, water)
    Telephone (basic service)

    Total Fixed Expenses

Step 3: List Variable Expenses
    Clothing
    Food (at home and meals out)
    Home Furnishings/household supplies
    Transportation
    Entertainment
    Personal Allowances
    Other (toll calls, etc.)

    Total Variable Expenses

    Total All Expenses

Step 4: Comparison
    Total Cash Available (from Step 1)
    Less Total Expenses (from Step 3)

    Cash Balance

LESSON 7
BUSINESS DECISION MAKING: ARE THEY OUT TO GET YOU?

INTRODUCTION

It isn't unusual to hear someone proclaim, "I can't believe the price of this item. That company is just taking advantage of the consumer. They think they can charge these prices just so they can make huge profits!" While some business owners do take advantage of consumers and may charge high prices when goods are in short supply, this antibusiness feeling some consumers have about huge profits and unreasonable prices is rooted partly in ignorance. A recent Gallup Poll found that almost 70 percent of the American public thought U.S. corporations made more than 20 percent profit each year. In reality, the rate of return on investment in U.S. corporations ranges from 10 to 15 percent depending on the industry, and many businesses fail by having sustained losses rather than profits. Competitive markets and knowledgeable consumers help keep prices down.

This lesson helps students actively explore the nature of business in a market economy, and thus helps them arrive at an understanding about how businesses make decisions. They learn that businesses must consider the costs of producing a product as well as consumer demand for the product. They learn first hand that if they charge a higher price, they will sell less of their product (the law of demand). They also learn that profit is an important incentive to firms. By experiencing another point of view, students will come to their own conclusion about the question: Are they out to get you?

CONCEPTS

Productive resources
Natural resource
Human resources
Capital resources
Fixed cost
Variable cost
Total cost
Total revenue
Profit
Competition

CONTENT STANDARD

The hope of earning profit motivates business firms to incur the risks involved in producing goods and services for the market.

OBJECTIVES

◆ Identify factors of production required to produce a product.

◆ Classify expenses as fixed or variable.

◆ Calculate the total cost and cost per unit of a product.

◆ Explain that price is set in the market between buyers and sellers.

◆ Calculate expected profit as total revenue less total cost.

◆ Evaluate data and determine at which price profit is maximized.

◆ Draw conclusions about how price of the product was determined and the effects of competition.

◆ Discuss what other adjustments might be made to the product (quality, service, etc.)

LESSON DESCRIPTION

This lesson helps students understand that businesses must consider the costs of producing their products and how those costs affect their profits. Many teachers form elaborate classroom corporations in order to help their students gain an understanding of and appreciation for the business person's perspective. The class is involved in market research, product pricing, production, marketing, and distribution. Such corporations often require significant resources, planning, and production efforts. This lesson is designed for the teacher who wants to incorporate this information into the classroom without going through the lengthy and formal process of setting up a classroom corporation. Students play the role of a business manager of a cookie company. They go through the kinds of decisions business managers must make (can revise price, profit, service, quality, etc.). The lesson requires several days for students to do investigative work.

TIME REQUIRED

Two to four class periods.

MATERIALS

★ Activity 1, Estimating Costs of Production. Teachers may provide price information or have students collect prices as a homework assignment.

★ Activity 2, What's The Best Price?

PROCEDURE

1. As a motivating activity, bring in a batch of chocolate chip cookies for refreshments. Tell students that they are going to have an opportunity to make the same kinds of decisions that business people make. Ask students why people go into business. They will probably respond that it is to make money from things people want. Ask students how businesses make this money. (They produce a product or service. The business is entitled to the profit remaining after all expenses are paid.) Poll the class to find out how much profit they think the average business makes. If you have the video, *Famous Amos*, pass out the cookies while the students view the video. (The video shows how Famous Amos cookies originated and details various aspects of business decision making. The video is available through the Foundation for Teaching Economics, 260 Russell Blvd., Suite B, Davis, CA 95616 / 916-757-4630.)

2. Divide students into cooperative learning groups. Tell the students that they will form cookie companies. Their objective is to raise enough money to buy a pair of $45 rollerblade skates. Have each group come up with a company name. (*Note:* You may want to have the companies raise enough money for something more relevant to your students. For example, a short trip, or enough money for one person to attend a local college, university, or technical school for one semester including tuition, fees, books, and parking. Keep in mind that for expensive items the

students will have to produce an extremely large quantity of cookies.)

3. Have students list the ingredients and the tools they will need to produce cookies. Write these on the board and tell students that these are called *productive resources,* all natural resources, human resources, and human-made resources (capital) used in the production of goods and services. Be sure the list includes more than the basic ingredients. (They should recall from the video the costs Famous Amos incurred.) Tell students that the productive resources may be classified into three categories: *natural resources* are "gifts of nature"; they are present without human intervention. *Human resources* represent the quantity and quality of human effort directed toward producing goods and services. *Capital resources* are goods made by people and used to produce other goods and services. Examples of capital resources include buildings, tools, and both raw and semifinished materials. (Some teachers may prefer to use just two categories— labor and capital—since several textbooks combine natural resources with capital.) Ask students to group the factors listed on the board into similar categories, according to similar characteristics. Try to place a descriptive word as a heading for each grouping. Then try to place the group into the categories and label them as land or raw materials, labor, and capital.

For homework: Distribute Activity 1. Each group must find its own recipe for chocolate chip cookies. (Encourage groups to search cookbooks and family recipe or locate the recipe on a package of chocolate chips—the more variety among groups, the better.) The recipe should include the number of cookies per batch. Each group should fill in Columns 1 and 2 on Activity 1 for homework. Groups must bring their recipes to class along with price information for all ingredients. Remind them that they must also consider the cost of cookie sheets, bowls, and any tools or equipment they will need. Their lists should be similar to the one developed on the board. Data may be obtained by visiting or phoning local stores or by searching cabinets at home. Be sure to tell students that if they phone a store they should explain they are collecting information for a class project. Set an appropriate deadline that allows ample time for groups to collect the data.

4. Explain to students that some costs change or vary with the number of cookies they make. Ask them to identify items on their list that are considered *variable costs*. (flour, salt, sugar, shortening, butter, chocolate chips, eggs, packaging, wages, etc.) You should also include one they will probably forget, electricity. The local power company has information on how much it costs to use an electric range for one hour. Add this cost to the list.

Next, explain that *fixed costs* are costs that do not change with the amount of a product produced. List these items on the board as students brainstorm the fixed costs of producing chocolate chip cookies. (mixing bowl, spoons, cookie sheets, measuring spoons, measuring cups, spatula, cooling racks, rent, insurance, etc.) Indicate that there are many fixed costs. For the purpose of this exercise, the costs will be limited to only those listed on the handout.

Explain that the *total cost* of producing a product is the sum of all costs, fixed and variable. Tell students that they will be asked to figure the total cost of producing one batch of cookies on Activity 1.

5. Refer to Activity 1. Each company should use the information from the homework assignment to complete the remainder of the handout. Tell students that in real situations there are other costs of doing business, which have not been included such as rent, insurance, and wages. (Students may need to review math skills necessary for calculating costs per batch from their price lists.)

Sample prices are provided below for one batch of chocolate chip cookies (Nestlé Toll House Recipe). These prices do not take into account the benefit of buying in large quantity or adding any special ingredients for a "gourmet" cookie:

Item	Price	Quantity	Cost
Variable Costs:			
Flour	5 pounds @ $1.49	1 cup + 2 Tbsp	$ .15
baking soda	1 pound @ $.65	½ tsp	*
salt	26 oz. @ $.39	½ tsp	*
butter	1 pound @ $1.79	1 stick	.45
brown sugar	1 pound @ $.75	½ cup	.05
sugar	4 pounds @ $1.59	⅓ cup	.10
vanilla	2 oz @ $2.99	½ tsp	.13
egg	1 dozen @ $.85	1	.07
chocolate chips	6 oz. @ $1.49	6 oz. chips	1.49
nuts	½ cup @ $1.49	½ cup	1.49
electricity	$.002 per min.	30 min	.06
Fixed Costs:			
cookie sheet	$6.49 each	2	$12.98
mixing bowl	3 quart @ $5.19	1	5.19
mixing spoon	$1.55 each	1	1.55
measuring spoons	$.99 each	1	.99
measuring cups	$1.49 each	1	1.49

* less than $.01

6. Ask students to look at their cost per cookie. (The average cost using the prices above would be $1.09 per cookie. Students may have similar costs). Ask students how much they would charge for their cookies. (Answers will vary). Explain that *revenue* is the number of units sold multiplied by the price of the product.

As they offer prices, ask students to explain why they would charge that price. (Most will want to cover their costs and make a profit.)

Explain that *profit* is the difference between revenues and the costs entailed in producing or selling a good or service; it is a return for risk taking. (It is important to note that when economists calculate profit, they include all costs; that is, the opportunity cost of what you invest in your business. Most classroom corporations calculate profit as a percent of sales revenue and do not estimate opportunity costs. This is what economists call accounting profit. Economic profit will be equal to or, most likely, less than accounting profit. This lesson assumes that students do not invest in their business. If they do, an opportunity cost should be incorporated into their profit figures.)

Explain that competition is another important

factor to consider. The level of *competition* in a market is largely determined by the number of buyers and sellers in the market. There are several cookie companies in the school marketplace and many buyers. Active competition among sellers results in lower prices and profit levels.

7. Discuss the following:

A. What price would you need to charge for sales revenue to be 5% above your cost? (Have each company multiply its average cost per cookie by 1.05. This is a convenient way to calculate 5% above cost on each cookie. If the cost per cookie is $1.40, a price of $1.47 would need to be charged to make 5% above cost.)

B. Do you think other people would be willing to pay this price for their cookies. Why? (Remind students that they may think their cookies are indescribably delicious, but buyers may not be willing to pay a high price for their cookies.)

C. What could you do to find out how much people are willing to pay for your cookies? (Students could conduct a market survey to determine how many cookies people would buy at various prices.)

D. What could you do to bring down the cost of your cookies? (modify the recipe, improve your production methods to produce more cookies with the same resource inputs, buy ingredients in large quantities.)

8. Refer students to Activity 1. Ask which cost was higher, variable or fixed. (Fixed cost) Explain that fixed costs per unit (cookie) can be reduced if more cookies are produced. This would also allow the companies to set a more realistic price and still make a reasonable profit.

9. Distribute Activity 2. Tell students to complete Parts I, II, and III.

A. In Part I the companies use the information from Activity 1 to calculate the cost per cookie for one batch of cookies.

B. In Part II they repeat Steps 1–5 for 5 batches of cookies and answer the following questions:

1. What happened to the total cost when your company produced 5 batches rather than 1 batch? (*Increased*)

2. What happened to the cost per cookie when your company produced 5 batches rather than 1 batch? (*Decreased*)

3. What price would you charge per cookie for sales revenue to be 5% above your costs? (Cost per cookie x 1.05)

4. Would consumers be willing to pay that price for your cookies? Why or why not? (Answers will vary. Consumers have limited income. If the price is too high, consumers may buy cookies from other companies or buy other less expensive snacks.)

C. In Part III the companies continue to figure the costs of additional batches until you find the quantity of cookies that can be sold at a reasonable price and provide enough profit to buy a pair of $45 rollerblade skates. There is no one right answer for this section. The quantity and price will depend upon their cost figures. Since each group has a different recipe and probably different costs, the answers will vary among groups.

CLOSURE

Students should answer the following questions:

1. How many cookies would you need to make and sell to earn $45? (Answers will vary.)

2. At what price would you sell your cookies? (Answers will vary. If the prices are too high, the teacher should point out that they may not charge an unrealistic price.)

3. Do you think consumers would buy all of your cookies at that price? Why or why not?

4. What other services or sales techniques might your company use to encourage sales? (sell

in larger quantities or at wholesale clubs, special packaging, offering services such as free delivery, advertising, etc.)

EXTENSION

1. Have each management team make a class presentation based on the information in Activities 1 and 2. They should include a statement on the process they used to determine how many cookies would be produced and at what price the cookies would be sold. Encourage students to use visuals.

2. Ask each student to write a report or essay for their writing portfolio on the one of the following topics:

   A. How has your point of view about business decision making (production and pricing) changed after playing the role of a business manager.

   B. What effect does competition from other cookie companies have on your price? Would your decisions be different if you were the only cookie company?

   C. If you were a business person, how would you respond to a customer who claimed that business is out to get them?

3. This lesson could be used in conjunction with a classroom corporation. Have students take a market survey to determine the prices consumers are willing to pay for their cookies and present their findings on a graph. Have the students develop a business plan if they need to borrow money or decide to sell stock in their company. Be sure they understand that they will probably need to put up collateral for their loan.

4. Another activity would incorporate language arts into the lesson. Students could write, illustrate, and produce a cookbook featuring their collection of chocolate chip cookie recipes.

ACTIVITY 1
ESTIMATING COSTS OF PRODUCTION

Name _____

Company Name _____

1. Variable Costs. List all of the ingredients needed to make one batch of cookies:

Item, size, price	Cost/unit	Quantity/batch	Cost/batch
flour 5 lb @ $	/oz.	oz.	$

Total Variable Costs:

2. Fixed Costs. For simplicity, include only the cost of the following items. Your company may decide how many of each to purchase.

cookie sheet
mixing bowl
spoon
measuring cups
measuring spoons

Total Fixed Costs:

3. Total Cost. Add the variable and fixed costs to get the total cost of making one (1) batch of cookies

1 batch of cookies
Cost per cookie (total cost ÷ no./batch):
No. of cookies per batch

ACTIVITY 2
WHAT'S THE BEST PRICE?

Name _____

Company Name _____

PART I. Follow the steps below to find out the cost per cookie for one batch of cookies. Fill in the information on the first line of the table.

A. *Step 1 - The number of cookies*: This is determined by the number of batches. Begin with one (1) batch. (Example: 1 batch makes 24 cookies)

B. *Step 2 - Fixed costs*: Remember that fixed costs will be the same for all batches. Enter the total fixed cost from Activity 7-1 in this column. (Example: $22.20)

C. *Step 3 - Variable costs*: Enter the total variable cost from Activity 7-1 in this column. (Example: $3.99)

D. *Step 4 - Total cost*: Add fixed costs and variable costs from Steps 2 and 3. (Example: $22.20 + $3.99 = $26.19)

E. *Step 5 - Cost per cookie*: Divide the total cost by the number of cookies. (Example: $26.19 / 24 = $1.09)

Number of cookies	Fixed Costs	Variable Costs	Total Cost	Cost per Cookie

PART II. Repeat Steps 1–5 for 5 batches of cookies. Enter this information on Line 2 in the table above.

A. What happened to the total cost when your company produced 5 batches rather than 1 batch?

B. What happened to the cost per cookie when your company produced 5 batches rather than 1 batch?

C. What price would you have to charge for each cookie if your company wanted to cover expenses and make a 5% accounting profit? (Cost per cookie x 1.05)

Would consumers pay that price for your cookies? Why or why not?

ACTIVITY 2 (CONTINUED)

Name_____

PART III. Continue to figure the costs of additional batches until you find the quantity of cookies your company would need to sell at a reasonable price and make enough profit to buy a pair of $45 rollerblade skates. Answer the following questions in your group:

A. How many cookies would you need to make?

B. At what price would you sell your cookies?

C. Do you think consumers would buy all of your cookies at that price? Why?

D. What other services or sales techniques might your company use to encourage sales?

LESSON 8
THE ROLE OF GOVERNMENT: WHO NEEDS IT?

INTRODUCTION

Virtually all high school students participate in the economy by paying taxes. Most students pay sales taxes when they consume goods and services. Those who work may be subject to federal and state income tax withholding. It is important for students to recognize where tax dollars are spent. It is also important for students to ponder whether some of the services provided by government could be provided profitably by the private sector, thus avoiding the necessity of taxation and allowing competitive forces to regulate.

Federal, state, and local governments, like individuals, must make choices about resource allocation. Many people would like more services from government, but they should be aware of the costs involved. Increased government services impose costs on taxpayers and result in fewer resources available to private sector enterprises. Some government services are considered to be essential while others might be reduced or eliminated. Economic analysis can help citizens make informed decisions.

CONCEPTS

Role of government
Sources of taxes
Government services
Scarcity
Opportunity cost
Trade-offs

OBJECTIVES

◆ Recognize that high school students pay taxes and receive benefits from services provided by government.

◆ Identify major sources and uses of federal government taxes.

◆ Evaluate costs and benefits of services provided by local government.

◆ Apply the concepts of opportunity cost and trade-offs to a situation involving scarcity facing local government.

◆ Analyze a hypothetical dilemma of conflicting goals faced by politicians.

CONTENT STANDARD

Some goods and services are provided by the government.

LESSON DESCRIPTION

Students view transparencies showing (1) a comic strip featuring a teenage taxpayer and (2) data on sources of federal government receipts. They participate in a group activity where they decide where the federal government should spend its money, and contrast their decisions with actual federal spending data. They evaluate local government services using information from a local phone book. They take part in a simulation where they analyze a problem of scarce resources facing local government under two scenarios: first, with the goal of "doing what is best" for constituents, and second, with the goal of seeking reelection.

TIME REQUIRED

Approximately two class periods, depending on length of discussions.

MATERIALS

One transparency each of Visuals 1 and 2.
★ One copy for each student of Activities 1, 2, and 3.

PROCEDURE

The content and activities in this lesson are appropriate for low-achieving students, as well as for average and above-average students. However, you may wish to modify some of the vocabulary for low achievers.

1. Display Visual 1 and ask students to answer the discussion questions. Encourage students to think about services provided by government. Point out that many people who file tax returns receive

refunds from the government because more taxes than necessary were withheld from their paychecks.

2. Thoroughly review the three basic levels of government with students: federal, state, and local. Remind them that each level of government has its own sources of revenue and is responsible for providing different types of services. To emphasize the different levels of government, tell students (or write on the board or on a transparency) that sales taxes and property taxes are the major sources of both *state* and *local* government revenue. The major spending categories for *state* governments are welfare programs, education, and transportation. Education and public safety are the major spending categories for *local* governments. (This information varies by locality.) Display Visual 2, which indicates the sources of *federal* government taxes. Many students are surprised that corporate taxes comprise only about 10% of the total. Individual income taxes include taxes on income of partnerships and sole proprietorships. Note that sales taxes do not go to the federal government. Ask students to suggest what the federal government should do with the tax money it collects.

3. Assemble the class into small groups of three to five students. Give each student a copy of Activity 1. Tell students that this activity focuses on *federal* government spending categories. Read the instructions at the top of the page with students. Working in groups, ask each student to fill in percentages in the second column indicating what they think would be a reasonable or desirable allocation of federal government resources among the major spending categories listed. Their percentages should total 100. Members of each group need not reach consensus, but they should discuss their reasons together. Ask each group to determine which three spending categories they think should be allocated the most money, and which three spending categories they think should be allocated the least money.

4. When the groups have finished, ask a member of each group to summarize to the class the three categories where they would allocate the largest percentage of funds, and the three categories where they would allocate the smallest percentage of funds. Write these categories on the board. Discuss differences among groups.

5. Inform students that you will now tell them the actual percentages of federal government funds allocated to the budget categories in Activity 1. Ask students to insert these numbers in the third column: Administration of Justice, 1%; Agriculture, 1%; Education, 4%; Health and Medicare, 17%; Income Security, 14%; International Affairs, 1%; National Defense, 17%; Net Interest, 14%; Science, Energy, Natural Resources, 3%; Social Security, 21%; Transportation, 3%.
(Data adapted from *1994 Information Please Almanac*.) Solicit student comments about the differences between the numbers in columns 2 and 3.

6. Distribute a copy of Activity 2 to each student. (You may wish to substitute a copy of a page from your local phone book and adapt the questions on Activity 2, Page 2 as necessary.) Emphasize that this activity focuses on services provided by *local* government. Ask students to read through the phone book page and answer the questions that follow in their small groups.

7. Ask some students to report their answers to the questions on Activity 2 to the class. Possible discussion questions include: Why do you think the services you listed for Question 1 are important? Why do you think some of the services listed are unnecessary? Are there any services listed that you think are important even though you and your family don't use them directly?

8. Distribute a copy of Activity 3 to each student. Tell students that this activity requires them to imagine that they are members of a city council in a town called Laurel Grove, a midsized city in the United States. Say:

"You have the power to decide how to spend local tax revenues. You have $5,000,000 to spend on 8 projects, all desired by people who live in Laurel Grove. Laurel Grove is a mid-sized city with average crime rates. The population includes many young families as well as many retired citizens. Current services provided by the city are considered by most to be "adequate," however, people would like improvements in many areas. The projects

must be funded in full or not at all. The estimated cost of each project is $1,000,000. You are unable to cut costs on these projects, and unable to collect additional revenues. Imagine that you are trying to make the best choices for the people of Laurel Grove. Which 5 projects will you fund?"

Ask students to reach consensus within their small groups about the 5 most-preferred projects. For reinforcement of prior learning, this activity could be done using a Decision Grid like the one introduced in Lesson 2.

9. When students have made their decisions, ask a member of each group to report their choices to the class. Make a list of the eight programs on the board, and tally how many groups chose to fund each project. Carefully discuss the reasons (criteria) that were used to make choices, and write the reasons on the board. Point out that the necessity of making choices results from the problem of scarcity faced by this local government. Discuss the opportunity costs of the decisions made.

10. Tell students that they will now repeat Activity 3, but that they will now choose 5 projects using only 1 criterion: as members of the city council, their only goal is to be reelected to office. Therefore, students should choose the five projects that will help them achieve this goal.

11. When students have made their decisions, tally how many groups chose to fund each project using the reelection goal as the only criterion. If different projects were chosen compared to the first time the activity was done, discuss the possible reasons for this.

CLOSURE

Several extensions and adaptations may be made to the activities presented in this lesson. After showing Visual 1, students could be taught how to fill in a simple tax return such as a 1040EZ. A sample W-2 could be displayed on a transparency (perhaps provided by a student in the class). The data in Visual 2 and Activity 1 could easily be updated using a current almanac. You could also compare current tax and spending priorities with those in past decades to show changes over time. As stated in Procedure 6, Activity 2 could be done using a telephone book from your locality. It could also be extended by adding the state and federal government phone book pages, and by making a transparency to show sources of local and state taxes. Activity 3 could be expanded by a more thorough discussion of public choice economics. You could also add to or adapt the choices in Activity 3 to make them relevant to your community.

VISUAL 1

Questions for discussion:

1. Why do young workers pay income taxes?

2. What other taxes do young people pay?

3. Why should Brad (in the cartoon) file his tax return?

4. What has the government done for you lately?

VISUAL 2
WHAT TAXES ARE COLLECTED BY THE FEDERAL GOVERNMENT?

INDIVIDUAL INCOME TAXES   45%

CORPORATE INCOME TAXES   10%

SOCIAL INSURANCE TAXES
AND CONTRIBUTIONS   37%

OTHER (includes estate, gift, customs taxes)   8%

Data adapted from *1994 Information Please* Almanac, page 55

From *Personal Decision Making: Focus on Economics,* © National Council on Economic Education, New York, NY

ACTIVITY 1
WHERE DOES THE FEDERAL GOVERNMENT SPEND THE MONEY?

Name _____

Twelve of the major categories of federal government spending are listed below. Next to each category are two lines. Decide what percentage of the federal budget you think *should* be allocated to each category. Write that number on the first line next to each budget category. (The category "other" has been filled in for you.) When you are finished, your teacher will tell you the percentage that the government actually allocates to that category. Write that amount on the second line.

BUDGET CATEGORY	Where *Should* the Money Go?	Where *Does* the Money Go?
Administration of Justice (includes federal courts)	_____%	_____%
Agriculture	_____%	_____%
Education	_____%	_____%
Health and Medicare	_____%	_____%
Income Security (includes welfare)	_____%	_____%
International Affairs (includes foreign aid)	_____%	_____%
National Defense	_____%	_____%
Net Interest (mainly interest paid on national debt)	_____%	_____%
Science, Energy, Natural Resources	_____%	_____%
Social Security	_____%	_____%
Transportation	_____%	_____%
Other	2 %	2 %
TOTAL	**100%**	**100%**

ACTIVITY 2
LOCAL GOVERNMENT SERVICES

Name _____

A good way to become familiar with the services your local government provides is to look at the government pages in your phone book. Look at the telephone book page here. Then look at your local telephone directory to identify federal, state, and local government services. Then answer the questions that follow.

10　　　　　　　　　　　　　　　**GOVERNMENT PAGES**

City Government Offices

Continued From Previous Page
MAYOR'S OFC—
Constituency Affairs Ofcs 51 Chambers	788-7585
Contracts Ofc Of 17 John	788-0010
Disabilities Ofc For People With 52 Chambers	788-2830
Drug Abuse Policy Ofc Of 52 Chambers	788-7494
Education Svces Ofc Of 250 Broadway	788-6719
Film Theater & Broadcasting 254 W 54	489-6710
Homelessness & Sro Housing Svces	
52 Chambers	788-2784
Housing Coordination Ofc Of 52 Chambers	788-2752
Increase The Peace Corps 253 Broadway	240-6877
Industrial Technology Assistance Corp	
253 Broadway	240-6920
Judiciary-Mayor's Comm On 36 W 44	944-6225
Loft Board 1 Centre St	669-4373
Mayor's Committee On Appointments 36 W 44	944-6454
Midtown Enfrcmnt Ofc Of 330 W 42	760-3550
Operations Ofc Of 100 Church	788-1400
Public Finance 110 William	513-6350
Public-Private Partnerships Ofc Of	
253 Broadway	240-4300
Second Careers Volunteer Program 51	
Chambers	566-1808
Street Activity Permit Ofc-CAU 51 Chambers	788-7438
United Nations-NYC Comm For The 2 UN Plaza	319-9300
Voluntary Action Center Mayor's Ofc	
61 Chambers	788-7580
Voter's Assistance Comm	788-8384
Women Commission On Status Of 52 Chambers	788-2738
Children & Families Ofc For 52 Chambers	788-6739

MENTAL HEALTH-MENTAL RETARDATION & ALCOHOLISM SVCES DEPT OF—
Bronx 93 Worth	566-1902
Brooklyn	718 643-4620
Bur Of Alcoholism 32 Broadway	487-3920
Commissioner's Ofc	334-2081
Information & Referral Svces 93 Worth	566-5222
Manhattan	566-7248
Mental Retardation Bur Of 93 Worth	925-6680
Prison Mental Health 311 Bway	285-4604
Staten Island	718 643-4620
Ofc Of Psychiatry 305 Bway	433-3036

METROPOLITAN MUSEUM OF ART 5 Av & 82—
Adult & College Group Appointments 1000 5 Av	570-3930
Branch—	
The Cloisters Fort Tryon Pk Manhattan	923-3700
Concerts & Lectures	570-3949
Offices	879-5500
Restaurant Reservations	570-3964
Retail Gift Shops	570-3726
School Groups (Grades K-12) Appointments	
1000 5 Av	288-7733
Tourist Groups Appointments	570-3711

MOLLEN COMMISSION 17 Battery Pl | 487-7350
MUNICIPAL BROADCASTING SYSTEM W N Y C
　SEE GENERAL SVCES DEPT OF
MUNICIPAL LABOR RELATIONS OFC OF
　110 Church—
Genl Information	618-8400
Managmnt Benefits Funds	788-1583
Medicare Reimbursement	385-1378
Main	618-8400

MUNICIPAL SUPLS DIV OF ......SEE GENERAL SVCES DEPT OF
MUSEUMS—
　American Museum Of Natural History

O

OFFICE OF LABOR RELATIONS—
General Information	306-7200
Deferred Compensation	306-7380

OMBUDSMAN-COUNCIL PRESIDENT | 669-7635
　Senior Action Line-Council President 1 Centre St | 669-7670
OPERATION GREENTHUMB 49 Chambers | 233-2926

P

PARKING VIOLATIONS BUR—
Genl Information Help-Line	477-4430
Update Information Recording	995-5133
NYC Sheriff's Ofc Scoff-Tow Or Boot	788-8759
All Other Tow Or Boot	788-7800

PARKS & RECREATION DEPT OF—
The Arsenal—
Headquarters-Central Park	360-8111
Budget & Fiscal Managmnt	360-8265
Citywide Svces	360-1316
Concessions	360-3405
Counsel	360-8257
Cultural & Historic Properties	360-3456
Operations	360-1307
Park Historian	360-3410
Parklands	360-3411
Press Office	360-8141
Program Audit	360-8221

Arsenal North—
Horticulture	360-1410
Natural Resources	360-1427
Recreation	360-2710
Recreation Services—	
REACH Program	718 699-4213
Sports & Fitness-Citywide—	
Basketball	860-1379
Golf	860-1317
Paddle Ball	360-2710
Track & Field	360-2713

Arsenal West—
16 West 61	830-7700
Management Information Systems	830-7911
Payroll & Timekeeping	830-7811
Personnel	830-7851
Purchasing & Accting	830-7951
Recruitment	830-7854

Borough Hdqtrs Info & Svces—
Complaints 9 AM-5 PM	408-0238
Manh Borough Svces-24 Hrs	408-0100

Central Park—
Belvedere Castle	772-0210
Central Park Conservancy	315-0385
Central Park Information	360-3456
Central Park Volunteers	360-2751
Charles A Dana Discovery Center	360-3456
Community Relations	860-1800
Dairy Visitor Center	794-6564
Facility Rentals	794-6564
Lasker Ice Skating Rink	996-1184
Maintenance & Operations	
E 79 & Tranverse Rd	628-1036
Maintenance & Operations Evenings And	

Continued From Previous Column
PARKS & RECREATION DEPT OF—
Recreation Centers—
Carmine Street	242-5228
East 54 St 348 E 54	397-3154
Highbridge W 173 & Amstrdm Av	927-9737
J Rozier Hansborough 35 W 134	234-9603
Jackie Robinson	234-9607
North Meadow	348-4867
Pelham Fritz E 122 & Mt Morris Park W	860-1377
West 59 St 533 W 59	397-3166

Senior Citizen Centers—
J Hood Wright Ft Washington Av & W 174	927-1539
Roosevelt Golden Age Center 80 Delancey	387-7680

Special Events Information Citywide-Recording | 360-3456
Stadia—
Downing Stadium Randalls Isl	860-1828
Permit Information	360-2713

Swimming Pools—
Hamilton Fish 127 Pitt	408-0100
Indoor-Labor Day To Close Of School Year—	
Asser Levey FDR Dr & Asser Levy Pl	447-2020
Carmine St 32 Carmine	242-5228
East 54 St (Open All Year) 348 E 54	397-3154
Rozier Hansborough-Open All Year	234-9603
W 59 St 533 W 59th	397-3159
Outdoor-Open End Of School Year To Labor	
Day—	
Asser Levey E 23 & Asser Levy Pl	447-2020
Carmine St 32 Carmine	242-5228
Dry Dock 408 E 10	677-4481
Highbridge W 173 & Amstrdm Av	927-2400
Jackie Robinson	234-9606
John Jay E 77 & York Av	794-6566
Lasker Pool 63 W 110	534-7639
Marcus Garvey 13 E 124	410-2818
Sheltering Arms W 129 & Amsterdam Av	662-6191
Susan E Wagner 350 E 124	534-4238
Thomas Jefferson	860-1372
W 59 St 533 W 59th	397-3159

Mini-Pools—
Information 16 W 61	408-0100

Technical Services—
Randalls Island	410-8900

Track—
East River Park FDR Dr & E 6	529-7185

Twenty Four Hour Parks Information-Complaint
Hotline
Toll Free-Dial '1' & Then	800 834-3832

TDD Twenty Four Hour Parks Information
Hotline
Toll Free-Dial '1' & Then	800 281-5722

Urban Park Rangers | 427-4040
Volunteers—
Citywide	360-1330
Manhattan	408-0214

Zoos—
Central Park Zoo Central Park	861-6030

PAYROLL ADMINISTRATION OFC OF
Municipal Bldg	669-8555

PEOPLE WITH DISABILITIES 52 Chambers | 788-2830
PERSONNEL DEPT OF—
Applications & Filing 18 Washington	487-6455
Eligibility Lists Info	487-6548
Examinations 2 Washington	487-6300
Medical Examinations 2 Washington	487-6594

ACTIVITY 2 (CONTINUED)

Name_____

1. List the five services that you think are most important on the government page shown from the telephone book or from your local telephone directory.

    1.

    2.

    3.

    4.

    5.

2. Are there any services listed that you think are unnecessary? If so, what are they?

3. Are there any services provided by government that you think could be provided profitably by private businesses, rather than with taxes collected by the city? If so, what are they?

4. Imagine that your list covers services provided by *your* local government or use the list made from your local directory. Which of the services provided have you or your family used in the past six months?

ACTIVITY 3:
THE CITY COUNCIL'S DILEMMA

Name _____

COMPUTERIZE POLICE NETWORK

$1,000,000 allocated to this program would improve the use of current police resources by computerizing the currently outmoded police dispatch services. With an advanced computer network, dispatchers would automatically know the location of all police vehicles at all times. This would decrease police response time to crime scenes by 50%. Police force employees claim that this would save lives and reduce injuries from violent crimes, as well as deter crimes.

FIRE PARAMEDIC PROGRAM

$1,000,000 allocated to this program would be used to hire and train paramedics so that a paramedic could be dispatched with every fire truck to the scenes of fires and other emergencies. Firefighters claim that this would result in saving lives and reducing the severity of traumatic injuries. It could also save money on the cost of ambulances since the paramedics would provide some ambulance-type services.

BUILD PUBLIC GOLF COURSE AND SWIM CENTER

$1,000,000 allocated to this program would provide a public golf course and swimming pool on public land. Recreational activities are somewhat limited in Laurel Grove, and there is widespread political support for this project. Retired citizens are especially in favor of the golf course, and have allied with young families who support the swimming pool. These groups speak loudly in favor of the golf course and swimming pool at weekly city council meetings, and have presented many petitions showing support for the projects.

REPAIR CITY ROADS AND BUILDINGS

$1,000,000 allocated to this program would allow the city to provide needed repairs to roads and public buildings, including police and fire department buildings and the historic city hall. Roads have many dangerous potholes and cracks in the pavement. Buildings have leaky roofs, peeling paint, and dangerous wiring. Repairs now would save money on repairs in the long run. Repairs now may also prevent expensive lawsuits from being filed against the city (which would have to be defended with tax revenues) if someone were hurt due to unsafe conditions.

PROVIDE PRENATAL AND NEONATAL MEDICAL SERVICES

$1,000,000 allocated to this program would provide medical services to expectant parents and newborn infants who have no other access to health care. Research studies indicate that women who receive regular medical checkups during pregnancy give birth to healthier babies than those who do not. Babies who are healthier at birth and receive checkups in infancy have better chances of success later in life, other things being equal. This program would prevent needless suffering of innocent babies and prevent expensive avoidable long-run medical treatment.

ACTIVITY 3 (CONTINUED)

Name _____

MODIFY FREEWAY INTERCHANGE TO ALLOW DEVELOPMENT OF SHOPPING MALL

$1,000,000 allocated to this program would allow a shopping mall to be built within Laurel Grove city limits. The existing freeway must be expanded to meet state standards before developers can build a mall, and developers have indicated that they will build the mall somewhere else if they have to pay for the freeway modification. Residents of Laurel Grove currently drive 20 miles to the nearest shopping mall in Pine Grove, and therefore all the sales tax revenues from the mall are collected by the city of Pine Grove. A shopping mall in Laurel Grove would be convenient for consumers, provide needed sales tax revenues to Laurel Grove, provide jobs for Laurel Grove residents, and reduce time spent driving on freeways (and the resultant pollution).

PROVIDE TAX BREAKS FOR A-1 MICROCHIP COMPANY

$1,000,000 allocated to this program would result in the A-1 Microchip Company continuing to operate in Laurel Grove. Currently, A-1 Microchip is the largest employer in Laurel Grove. Many citizens are employed there as researchers, engineers, technicians, and assemblers. Due to a recent recession and foreign competition, the factory is currently operating at a loss. A-1 management has announced that it will have to shut down unless the city of Laurel Grove forgives $1,000,000 in business and property taxes that A-1 owes.

ESTABLISH YOUTH SERVICE CORPS

$1,000,000 allocated to this program would hire high school and college students to provide services to needy citizens in Laurel Grove. Hot meals would be prepared and delivered to the sick and elderly, children from poor families would receive after-school tutoring, and handicapped citizens would be provided with rides and assistance with chores that they are unable to perform themselves. Along with helping those in need, this program would help solve a large youth unemployment problem, while providing young people with both money and job training.

LESSON 9
COLLECTIVE BARGAINING: A NEGOTIATION SIMULATION

INTRODUCTION

Scarcity is perhaps the most important concept in economics. Scarcity is the relationship between wants and limited resources that are insufficient to fulfill those wants. The result: we cannot have everything we want. In this lesson, students discover that labor and management both face scarcity, and that they depend upon each other to accomplish two goals, production and employment. As with all situations involving scarcity, neither labor nor management can have everything it wants; a trade-off is involved in every decision.

Most decisions are not "all or nothing," they involve a little bit of "give" in one place and a little bit of "take" in another place. It is this "little bit" that economists call the margin. Negotiations of all types involve decisions at the margin. In this lesson, the concepts of scarcity, trade-off, and marginal analysis help students negotiate a contract. While the exercise focuses on a formal union/management contract, these types of negotiations are also common in less formal settings when two people or groups who depend upon each other try to reach an agreement that is mutually beneficial, but in which neither party gets all that it wants.

CONCEPTS

Interdependence
Scarcity
Trade-off
Marginal cost
Marginal benefit

CONTENT STANDARD

Few choices are all-or-nothing propositions. They usually involve trade-offs, that is, getting a little more of one option in exchange for a little less of something else.

OBJECTIVES

◆ Identify the interdependence of labor and management.

◆ Identify scarcity faced by both labor and management.

◆ Make trade-offs in a negotiating session.

◆ Use marginal cost/benefit analysis to negotiate a labor contract.

LESSON DESCRIPTION

Students will form labor and management teams to negotiate a contract. Two bargaining sessions take place, at the end of which a contract is negotiated or a strike or a lockout occurs.

TIME REQUIRED

Five class periods.
Day 1. Explanation of concepts, original student essays, distribution of activity, original strategy session.
Day 2. First negotiation session.
Day 3. Strategy session.
Day 4. Final negotiating session.
Day 5. Reports by groups, debriefing, assignment of final essay.

MATERIALS

★ One copy for each student of Activity 1(Management) or Activity 3 (Labor)
★ Activity 2, Negotiating Worksheet, for each student
★ Activity 4, Negotiating Worksheet, for each student

PROCEDURE

DAY ONE

1. Explain the basic concepts. Scarcity results from the basic relationship between relatively unlimited wants and limited resources. Labor unions and business firms face scarcity directly. A trade-off is the process whereby you give up something of value in order to get something else. In a labor bargaining session there are always examples of trade-offs. Perhaps the union can get

★ all students–basic course material
■ average and above average students

another paid holiday for its members, but to get this benefit, the members may have to give up some medical benefits. It is important for students to understand that very few decisions are "all or nothing." Most decisions involve a little more or a little less. Economists call these "marginal" decisions. Tell students that they will use these concepts in the next three days to negotiate a contract between management and labor.

2. Have students write a one paragraph answer to each of these questions.

   A. What are the goals and limits of a union?

   B. What are the goals and limits of the management of a firm?

   C. How do labor and management depend upon each other?

   D. What limits do labor and management face in negotiating a contract?

Save these paragraphs for later discussion. (The purpose of this part of the lesson is to get students' general impressions of labor and management and to contrast them with what should be their more knowledgeable impressions after the lesson.)

3. Divide the class in half; half the students will be labor and half will be management. Divide both halves into teams of four, five, or six. If you have a class of 36, for example, you would have three management teams and three labor teams of six each. There are five issues to be resolved: wages, job security, child care, medical benefits, and an additional holiday. Ideally, on each team, there will be one member who is responsible for each issue and one member who is the chief negotiator. In most cases, however, teams may have four or five members, requiring that some team members have more than one issue with which to deal.

4. Present the following scenario to the class:

A manufacturing company and a labor union are about to negotiate a contract. The position of both parties is outlined in the following activity.

5. Distribute Activity 1(Management) to the management teams and Activity 1 (Labor) to the labor teams. Explain that these activities explain the situation and positions of each side. The second part of the activity explains how much each marginal wage increase will cost management if they are granted and labor if they are not granted. (Notice that the units of cost for management are dollars and the units of cost for labor are "strike probability.") Finally, instructions are given regarding the negotiation process. Give each team the rest of the period to prepare their bargaining positions.

DAY TWO

6. Set up the management and labor teams for negotiating sessions. Give them one-half hour to negotiate an interim agreement.

7. Have a spokesperson from each group explain where they stand and how close they are to reaching agreement. Have them explain how the process worked and how they agreed on certain issues. Have one management group and one labor group report.

DAY THREE

8. In a strategy session, have each team adjust their position to reflect the results of the first bargaining session. This time should be used to prepare for the final round of negotiations.

DAY FOUR

9. Give the students the entire class to reach a final agreement. If they fail to reach an agreement, they must go to binding arbitration where you are the final arbiter. This is not an optimal situation. Have one labor group and one management group explain their final agreement and the process by which they reached agreement. While there is no set answer to this exercise, both parties should give up those things that have the best marginal benefit/marginal cost ratios for them. Allow students to come up with different types of bargaining on particular issues that are not listed here.

CLOSURE
DAY FIVE

10. Have each team report on the results of their negotiations. Make copies of each side's worksheets and have each side explain to the other side exactly what constraints they faced and how close they came to the original plans. Have each management team calculate their profits and present them to the union team. Have each union team report on the difference between a 100% strike probability and their final result.

Emphasize the fact that management and labor depend upon each other, as do all buyers and sellers of resources and products. Both sides face scarcity and the use of marginal analysis (gaining a little and giving up a little) enables individuals and groups to deal with scarcity more efficiently.

ASSESSMENT

11. As a homework assignment, have each student answer the questions that they answered originally,

   A. Describe the goals and limits of a union.

   B. Describe the goals and limits of the management of a firm.

   C. How do labor and management depend upon each other?

   D. What limits do labor and management face in negotiating a contract?

12. After the essays have been submitted and graded, give the students their original answers to the four questions. Have them compare the two sets of answers and write a one-page essay explaining what they learned from this exercise. In this final essay, they should use the terms *scarcity, interdependence, trade-offs,* and *marginal cost/benefit analysis.*

ACTIVITY 1
MANAGEMENT

Name _____

Your position. The Company can afford approximately $1 million. Any more and you will be unable to compete with foreign competition; you will be forced to close the doors. Workers are productive, management positions have been cut, the company has streamlined and is currently keeping the stockholders reasonably happy. Your resources are fixed. At this time, $1 million is the most that you can afford. You very much want to avoid a strike since it is likely to cost the company $200,000 and you will then have to begin the negotiations all over again. Labor does not know your $1 million constraint. You may choose to reveal it or not. The number in parentheses is the additional labor costs per hour of each demand.

Total Funds Available for this contract: $1 million	
ISSUE	COST IF LABOR'S DEMAND IS NOT MET
Wages	$1 million (70 cents per hour)
Job Security	$200,000 (14 cents per hour)
Child Care	$1 million (70 cents per hour)
Medical	$240,000 (16.8 cents per hour)
Holiday	$50,000 (3.5 cents per hour)
Total Value of Labor's Initial Demands	**$2,490,000**

The Issues (Management)

Wages. As always, this is one of the two most important issues to the workers and to the company. Workers feel that they have taken very small wage increases in the past. While management has made some sacrifices, there have not been many salary cuts at the top. The workers feel that they are entitled to an 8% increase.
You are aware that this is an important issue. The problem is that the entire 8% would cost you $1 million, leaving room for no further concessions. Each 1% increase costs $125,000. An optimal deal might include a 3% raise, which would cost $375,000, leaving room for negotiations in other areas. This is likely to be a difficult area where you may have to give more than you would like.

Job security. The company has been trying to hire nonunion, part-time workers to avoid benefits and overtime. Labor wants to prevent this since the company does not then hire union workers. Next to wages, job security is the single biggest issue for the workers.
You need to have some flexibility in hiring part-time workers. It is your money and you should be able to hire anyone you want. More important, it is tough to know whether an increase in business is a temporary deal or a long-term increase. If you hire some full-time workers and then have to lay them off, the union will go crazy. There is, of course, the additional benefit that you don't have to pay benefits to part-time workers and you will save a great deal of overtime. This year that will save the company $200,000.

ACTIVITY 1 (CONTINUED)

Name_____

Child care. The union has been pushing for child care for quite a while with no success. Either a child care facility on the premises or paid child care would be acceptable to the members.

It is not now, nor has it ever been the responsibility of a company to care for a worker's children. This is a little bit ridiculous. Pretty soon management will be asked to give the children away at weddings and come to their graduations. Business is business, it is the responsibility of families to care for their children. If they want day care, there are plenty of good facilities available to them.

Medical. The company provides a good medical care program but its cost is rising dramatically. If the cost increase continues, you feel that you will soon be unable to provide the same level of benefits as in the past. You would like labor to share in the increased costs.

Another paid holiday. Both men and women in the union are pushing for another paid holiday, their birthdays. While another holiday may not cost much in extra expenses the company will have to bring in temporary workers in some departments.

Workers already receive 10 paid holidays per year, as much or more than comparable businesses. This, however, would cost relatively little to give up and should be thrown on the table at some point.

Your situation. You realize that the union has some legitimate demands and both of you would like to avoid a strike. Nevertheless, any package that costs you more than $1 million will put you out of business. Scarcity is staring you in the face. What package can you put together that will minimize the chances of a strike while keeping within your budget constraints? Do not reveal your final position to labor at the beginning of the negotiations. Recognize that you will have to respond to labor by giving in on some issues. Attempt to give in on the issues that have the lowest marginal cost to you with the highest marginal gain for labor. You can give in to some demands partially. Use flexibility and imagination in preparing your offers. While your total package cannot cost more than $1 million, a little breathing room would be nice. If you could negotiate a $750,000 final agreement, management would sleep better. You may want to act "hard-nosed", but you do want to avoid a strike. Your negotiating skills will be important in determining how costly this agreement is to you.

Your tasks. There will be two rounds of negotiations. You are going to work backwards, using the negotiating worksheet to prepare three positions on the issues.

ACTIVITY 2
NEGOTIATING WORKSHEET (MANAGEMENT)

Name _____

Issue	Desired Final agreement	Labor's Initial Demand	Your Response to Labor's Initial Demand	Your Position After Round 1	Labor's Position After Round 1	Bargaining Position for Round 2	Final Agreement
Wages							
Job Security							
Child Care							
Medical							
Holiday							
Total Cost							

Use the negotiating worksheet and complete a final agreement that would avoid a strike and keep the company from bankruptcy. This is the best deal that you can reasonably hope to gain.

1. Prepare an initial response to labor's demands that will move you in the direction you would like to go.

2. After the first negotiating session, record the positions of you and labor. Prepare a set of concessions for the second round of negotiations.

3. After you have, hopefully, reached agreement, record your final position. How close did you come to the desired final position that you originally planned?

ACTIVITY 3
LABOR

Name _____

Your position. The company has been doing reasonably well. Profits have been growing. While the company has downsized its management team, it has also laid off some workers and wage increases have been minimal. It is time to play catch-up. You can ill afford a strike. Your strike fund will last only about 10 days.

Issue	Contribution to Strike Probability if not met
Wages	50%
Job Security	30%
Child Care	10%
Medical	20%
Holiday	30%
Total Strike Probability if no demands are met	140%

Marginal Cost of Not Gaining Wage Increase	
Marginal Wage Demand	**Strike Probability if Not Met**
First 3%	40%
Next 2%	7%
Next 3%	3%

THE ISSUES (LABOR)

Wages. As always, this is one of the two most important issues to the workers and to the company. You feel that you have taken very small wage increases in the past. While management has made some sacrifices, there have not been many salary cuts at the top. The workers feel that they are entitled to an 8% increase.

This is a big one. Some wage increase is an absolute must. The amount of increase is negotiable. The table above presents the probability of a strike with a 3%, 5%, and 8% increase. With no wage increase, the probability of a strike is 50%. The first 3% increase reduces that probability by 40% to 10%. The next 2% reduces the probability by 7% to 3%, and the next 3%

reduces the probability to 0 on the wage issue.

Job security. The company has been trying to hire nonunion, part-time workers to avoid benefits and overtime. Labor wants to prevent this since the company does not then hire union workers. Next to wages, job security is the single biggest issue from the perspective of the workers.

This is one more way that the company avoids rewarding labor for years of loyalty and hard work. It is better for the company to pay experienced workers overtime since they are more productive than new, part-time workers. If you allow the hiring of part-timers, there is a fear that the company will lay everyone off and then hire them back on a part-time basis. This is a major threat to job security.

 From *Personal Decision Making: Focus on Economics,* © National Council on Economic Education, New York, NY

ACTIVITY 3 (CONTINUED)

Name _____

Child care. The union has been pushing for child care for quite a while with no success. Either a child care facility on the premises or paid child care would be acceptable to the members.

The old days are gone forever, or should be. It now takes two workers to keep a family's head above water. With most women working, the company needs to address the new situation. If a family is required to pay child care, it is almost not worth one of the parents working. (This is not as important an issue as others. It will happen, but the membership is not as excited about this in these negotiations.) Female members have been becoming more and more adamant about this issue. Failure to address it will cause both labor union leadership and management to appear to be ignoring women's issues.

Medical. The company provides a good medical care program but its cost is rising dramatically. If the cost increase continues, management claims that it will soon be unable to provide the same level of benefits as in the past. They would like labor to share in the increased costs. You see this as the opening of the floodgates and feel that you really can't give much on this issue.

Another paid holiday. Both men and women members are pushing for a new paid holiday on their birthday(or the nearest workday date). Given stress in the workplace they feel there should be another holiday for personal relaxation. Members believe management can afford this benefit because they think that, "just a few people away from the job each will not cost real dollars." But the issue is not as important to women, who compose about 25% of total membership, as is child care.

Your situation. Anything that brings the probability of a strike to 100% is a defeat for you. Your strike fund will not allow a long strike. You also recognize that the company has limited resources. You both face scarcity. Nevertheless, your workers have legitimate demands. Your company has fall-

en behind some others in the industry in terms of wages and benefits. Many of your members are living from paycheck to paycheck, unable to put anything away for financial security. This cannot be allowed to continue. You understand the company's financial situation and have no intention of driving them to bankruptcy, but your members need some relief.

What package can you put together that will maximize the benefits to the workers, minimizing the chances of a strike without driving the firm toward bankruptcy.

Do not give away your final positions at the beginning of the bargaining sessions. Your job is to get the best deal that you can. Recognize that you will have to respond to management by giving up some of your demands. Attempt to give in on the issues that have the highest marginal gain for the workers and the lowest marginal cost to management. You can give up some demands partially. Each demand is not an all-or-nothing issue. If you know that you cannot get all of a particular demand try for some of it. Every time you prepare a bargaining position, calculate the additional (marginal) strike probability of each marginal demand given up. You may want to act "hard-nosed," but you do want to avoid driving the firm out of business.

Your tasks. There will be two rounds of negotiations. You are going to work backward, preparing two positions in addition to the original demands.

1. List a final agreement that would avoid a strike and keep the company from bankruptcy. This is the best deal that you can reasonably hope to gain.
2. Prepare a bargaining position you would like to hold after the first round of negotiations.

ACTIVITY 4
NEGOTIATING WORKSHEET (LABOR)

Name _____

Issue	Desired Final agreement	Your Initial Demand	Mgmt's Response to Your Initial Demand	Your Position After Round 1	Mgmt's Position After Round 1	Bargaining Position for Round 2	Final Agreement
Wages							
Job Security							
Child Care							
Medical							
Holiday							
Total Cost Probability							

Use the negotiating worksheet and complete a final agreement that would avoid a strike and keep the company from bankruptcy. Prepare a final agreement that would satisfy many of your demands but is realistic for both sides.

1. After the first negotiating session, record your position and that of management.

2. In your conference, prepare a set of concessions for the second round of negotiations.

3. After you have, hopefully, reached agreement, record your final position. How close did you come to the desired final position that you originally planned?

LESSON 10
CONSUMER CREDIT: BUY NOW, PAY LATER, AND MORE

INTRODUCTION

The word credit comes from the Latin word *creditus* meaning *entrusted*. Credit means that someone will lend you money and give you time to pay it back, usually with interest. Credit allows you to buy now and pay later.

The introduction of credit cards in the economy has influenced the way consumers purchase goods and services. In 1993, Americans charged more than $350 billion on their credit cards and paid $36 billion in interest charges.[1] Despite the widespread use of credit cards, many consumers do not fully understand the terms, interest rates, and charges on their credit cards.

Each year the number of Americans who use credit cards increases. According to a survey by MasterCard International, 32 percent of high school students and 62 percent of college students had at least one credit card in 1993. The use of a credit card is a loan from the issuer of the card and not used in place of cash. If the amount owed on a credit card is paid in full each month, there is no additional cost for using the credit card. However, if the borrower is unable or unwilling to pay the credit card bill in full, there is an interest or finance charge on the unpaid balance. The effect of the finance charge is the increased cost of goods and services purchased with a charge card.

CONCEPTS

Credit
Consumer credit
Decision making
Opportunity cost
Interest

CONTENT STANDARD

Few choices are all-or-nothing propositions; they usually involve trade-offs, that is, getting a little more of one option in exchange for a little less of something else.

OBJECTIVES

◆ Determine the costs and benefits of using credit cards.

◆ Discuss and analyze the decision-making process when using credit cards.

◆ Identify ways and criteria to establish and obtain credit.

LESSON DESCRIPTION

Through group activity, students analyze the costs and benefits of using credit cards to purchase goods and services.

TIME REQUIRED

3 class periods.

MATERIALS

★ Copies of Activities 1, 2, 3, 4, and 5
Transparencies of Visuals 1, 2, 3, and 4

PROCEDURE

1. Divide students into cooperative learning groups. Explain that the purpose of the lesson is to learn the costs and benefits of using credit cards. Display Visual 1 and distribute Activity 1, Credit Card Fact Sheet.

2. Ask each group to share new information learned from the reading. List and discuss responses on the board. Ask students, "Why are more people using credit cards and paying monthly finance charges when that increases the price of the goods and services they buy?" Write student hypotheses on chart paper for future reference. (These hypotheses could include convenience, emergency, immediate benefit, defer cost of goods.)

3. Explain: (1) opportunity cost of purchasing goods and services with credit cards. (The opportunity cost is the value of whatever is given up

---

[1] *Financial Responsibility,* American Express, 1994
(Data compiled from *Nilson Report 563,* January 1994, 6-7, and *Lehman Global Economics,* 1993)

★ all students–basic course material
■ average and above average students

when you purchase an item with a credit card; the use of future income; and whatever else could have been bought with the interest payment.); (2) the collective cost of using credit. (If you continue to purchase goods or services with a credit card without paying the unpaid balance each month, the finance charge is computed on the total unpaid balance. This can increase the cost of the items purchased.); and (3) the use of credit cards for purchasing consumable and durable goods. (Generally, using credit cards to purchase living expenses such as clothing, groceries, gasoline and restaurant meals is not wise if you don't pay off your bill at the end of the month because you will pay more and you may use up the purchase before you repay the loan. However, if you pay off your bill at the end of each month, there is no additional cost for the consumable item. And you can use installment loans to finance large purchases such as automobiles or appliances because the interest rate is generally lower than rates for credit cards.)

4. Ask students, "Why don't people analyze all the cost(s) of using credit before their purchase?" Discuss and list student responses on the board.

5. Distribute Activity 2, Situations, and Activity 3, Planning Your Credit Purchase. Each group will have a situation to analyze. For each situation, the person named has a credit card and pays the minimum required at the end of the month. The credit card has an APR of 18% or 1.5% per month on the unpaid balance. Upon completion of Activity 3 planning matrix, each group will share its purchase decision with the class. To help students complete Activity 3, do one scenario with the class.

6. Display Visual 2, Benefits of Credit Cards, and Visual 3 Costs of Credit Cards. Discuss and give an example of each item on the lists. Summarize the benefits and costs of using credit cards.

7. Tell students the second part of this lesson is on how to obtain credit. Display Visual 3, The 3Cs of Credit. Discuss and explain the 3Cs, the criteria lenders use when issuing credit. These are *capacity,* your ability to pay back a loan; *col-*

lateral, your assets used as a guide to figure out your ability to repay the debt; and *character,* your reputation as a reliable and trustworthy person.

8. Ask, "Why are the 3Cs important?" (They help determine whether the borrower has the ability and willingness to repay the loan.) "How can you best show your ability to satisfy the requirements of the 3Cs?" (*Capacity,* employment, wages earned, monthly payments; *collateral,* assets such as a house, car, or other valuable items that could be sold to repay the debt; *character,* how you repaid other loans, stability, how long you have lived at our present address, rent or own your home).

9. Have groups discuss and list features of various credit cards to compare when shopping for the "best" credit card. (List may include: interest rate, grace period, annual fee or membership fee, credit limit, cash advance, acceptance by merchants, frequent flyer miles, discounts, or gifts).

CLOSURE

To conclude the lesson ask, "Why are more people using credit cards and paying monthly finance charges when the charges increase the effective price of the goods and services? What are the costs and benefits of purchasing goods and services with a credit card?" Refer to the student hypotheses at the beginning of the lesson.

Using A Credit Card

Benefits	Costs
Earlier consumption, use of goods while paying for them	Costs more if unpaid balance is not paid monthly
Convenience	Ties up future income
Use for emergencies	Tempts one to overspend
Establishment of credit history	Reduces comparison shopping if you shop only in stores extending you credit
Identification	Decreases future buying power

OPTIONAL ACTIVITY

1. Distribute Activity 4, Credit Card Usage Survey, for an outside class activity. Each group will survey 5 people representing various age groups to assess cardholder's knowledge of the cost(s) of using credit. The analysis of the survey is to be completed the next class period.

2. Each group will summarize the results of their survey. Discuss the findings. (The findings should reveal credit card use is high; however, most people are unfamiliar with the terms and costs of using their credit cards. Studies have shown that many people who don't pay off their bills every month will say that they do.)

Note: If your school is located in a low socioeconomic area or has a large immigrant population, it may be difficult to find high usage of credit cards due to income or cultural values. Then discuss, why is credit card usage low?

3. Ask, "Why do so many people continue to use credit cards when they do not know the financial and opportunity cost(s) of using them? What are the benefits of using a credit card? What are the costs of using a credit card?" List student responses on the board.

ACTIVITY 1
CREDIT CARD FACT SHEET

Name _____

The word credit originates from the Latin word *creditus* meaning *entrusted*. Credit means that someone will lend you money and give you time to pay it back, usually with *interest* (money paid for the use or borrowing of money). When purchasing goods and services with your credit card, you are getting a loan from the issuer of the credit card. It is not used in place of cash. Consumers use credit cards to buy things they want or need.

A credit card is a plastic card identifying the holder as a participant in a credit plan of a lender. Many stores and companies such as oil companies issue credit cards for use only at their place of business. Banks and other financial institutions issue credit cards, such as Visa or MasterCard, that can be used at any establishment that accepts credit cards.

Cardholders can purchase services, merchandise, or obtain cash advances (loans). Most credit cards are used as open-ended credit accounts or charge accounts, originally designed for the short-run money needs of consumers. These accounts have a credit limit (*the maximum amount you may charge)* and a flexible repayment schedule. The cardholder who pays the entire balance due within the grace period (*a period of time after the due date not subject to late charges)* avoids interest or finance charges. A *late charge* is a payment for not paying the balance owed before the due date. If a card offers a grace period, federal law requires a bill be sent to the cardholder at least 14 days before payment is due. A cardholder can repay any amount equal to or greater than the purchase price to eliminate interest charges.

A wise consumer will pay off credit card bills promptly. If you don't pay it off, you are taking out a loan and it can be very expensive. Would I take out a loan for dinner tonight? Avoid the minimum payment trap. People who pay the mini-

mum think they are handling their finances, but it could take them a long time to pay off the bill. Many cardholders maintain balances and the average customer takes more than 15 months to pay for the charges.[1] When a credit card is used responsibly, the cardholder can build a good credit history. If not, it can ruin a person's credit record. A bad credit record is hard to fix and takes many years to correct.

Sixty (60%) percent of all families make credit card purchases. Worldwide, more than 90 million MasterCard, 41 million Discover, and 142 million Visa cards are issued.[2] Credit cards are issued by local and national businesses as well as banks. With the passage of the Fair Credit and Charge Card Disclosure Act in 1988, credit card issuers must inform consumers before they sign up about: (1) annual percentage rate (APR), (2) how monthly fees are calculated, (3) cost of all fees such as membership, transaction, cash advance and others, and (4) grace period.

Not all plastic cards are credit cards. The use of bank debit cards and smart cards is increasing. The debit card automatically deducts money from checking accounts. The smart card stores valuable information about the consumer on computer chips instead of magnetic strips. This allows businesses access to better information about the consumer so that they can provide personalized service. Some consumers are concerned about privacy issues associated with smart cards and credit cards knowing so much about them.

Credit cards help consumers satisfy their wants and needs, but how does the credit card affect the issuers of cards and businesses that accept purchases made by credit cards? Purchases made by credit cards issued by banks charge merchants a transaction fee. This fee is a percentage of the price of any good or service purchased with a

---

[1] E. Thomas Garman. (1993). *Consumer Economic Issues in America.* Houston: DAME Publications.
[2] Ibid.

ACTIVITY 1 (CONTINUED)

Name _____

credit card. Credit card issuers charge interest on the unpaid balances not paid during the grace period and they may collect an annual fee from cardholders. American Express and other companies issue gold or platinum status credit cards. These cards may have higher annual fees, but include extras such as travel insurance and other benefits.

The prime target for credit companies is the "baby boom" generation. Families headed by younger persons use consumer credit more than families headed by older persons. Higher income groups use credit more than lower income groups. Some companies target a younger market and issue cards to college students. According to a survey by MasterCard International, 32 percent of high school students and 62 percent of college students had at least one credit card in 1993.

ACTIVITY 2
SITUATIONS

Name _____

Directions: For each situation listed below, complete questions on Activity 3, Planning Your Credit Purchase, to help determine the costs and/or benefits of a credit card purchase. In each situation, the person named has a credit card with an APR of 18% or 1.5% per month on the unpaid balance. Each person named also is expected to pay all credit card balances and fees

Situation 1

Jennifer is a senior in high school. Her parents gave her a credit card and told her that she may use the card only in case of an emergency. As she was walking across the Mall, she saw the perfect dress for the senior prom in a store window display. The prom is two weeks away. The tag on the dress was $125.00. Also on the window was a sign: **One day only, all items 25% off ticket price.** Jennifer's grandmother, a dressmaker, told her if she needed a special outfit, she would be willing to sew it for her. What should Jennifer do?

Situation 2

Tony spends much of each day in his car commuting from home to school and work. His parents gave him a credit card to be used only for emergencies. Recently, the radio in his car went on the blink. He enjoys listening to music on his long drives. He went to the repair shop and was told it would cost $75.00 to diagnose the problem. To fix the problem, he would have to pay additional costs for labor and parts. The repair person told Tony that his shop had a special sale on a portable CD player for $150.00. What should Tony do?

Situation 3

Sarah is a college student who had volunteered to drive three members of her debate team to the state debate championship in a city 75 miles away. As they were approaching a small town half way to their destination, they stopped at a fast-food restaurant to get something to eat. When they got back into the car, the car would not start. The girls got out and pushed the car to the gas station next door. Sarah was told her battery was dead and a new one would cost $80. If the girls pooled all their money, they would have just enough money to purchase the battery. Sarah could have the car jump-started and hope that the battery will recharge itself during the rest of the trip. The service station attendant will accept her credit card. Sarah is responsible for paying all her auto repair bills. What should Sarah do?

Situation 4

Jason is an honors pre-med student at the state university. He is on a very limited budget. Each semester, he charges his tuition and fees. He pays for his books with money in his savings account, which has only $30 left. One of his professors strongly recommended that he purchase books on an optional reading list that cost $250 to better prepare him for medical school entrance exams. A high score on the entrance exam may help Jason get a scholarship to attend medical school. What should Jason do?

ACTIVITY 3
PLANNING YOUR CREDIT PURCHASE

Name _____

What decision are you trying to make?	
What goals do you hope to accomplish in making your decision?	
What are the alternatives?	
List the *benefits* of the purchase with a credit card.	
List the *costs* of the purchase with a credit card:	
Make a decision • Which alternative best matches your goal? • What do you gain with each alternative? • What do you give up with each alternative?	

ACTIVITY 3
PLANNING YOUR CREDIT PURCHASE

Name _____

Situation 1

What decision are you trying to make?	*Determine the costs and benefits of purchasing a prom dress with a credit card.*
What goals do you hope to accomplish in making your decision?	*Have a dress for the prom.*
What are the alternatives?	*Don't buy the dress, look for another dress, ask Grandma to sew a dress.*
List the *benefits* of the purchase with a credit card.	*Take advantage of the sale price of the dress, don't have to spend time to look for another dress.*
List the *costs* of the purchase with a credit card:	*Cost of the dress plus the finance charge, Grandma's feelings may be hurt.*
Make a decision • Which alternative best matches your goal? • What do you gain with each alternative? • What do you give up with each alternative?	

ACTIVITY 4
CREDIT CARD USAGE SURVEY

Name _____

QUESTION	ANSWER
1. a. Do you have a credit card? b. Do you have more than five credit cards?	
2. a. Do you use your credit card once a week? b. Do you use your credit card more than once a week?	

3. a. Do you use your credit card for convenience?
   b. Do you use your credit card in emergencies?
   c. Do you use your credit card for identification?
   d. Do you use your credit card to consolidate debts?
   e. Do you use your credit card so you can use something before paying for an item?
   f. Do you use your credit card to establish a credit history?	

4. a. Do you purchase gas with a credit card?
   b. Do you purchase consumable goods with your credit card?
   c. Do you purchase durable goods with your credit card?	

5. a. Do you pay off your bill monthly?
   b. Do you pay the minimum each month?
   c. Do you pay a set amount each month?	

6. Estimate your monthly cost of using your credit cards.	
7. What is the annual percentage rate of your most used credit card?	
8. What is the annual membership fee of your most used credit card?	
9. What is the late charge on your most used credit card?	
10. What is your monthly credit card costs.	
11. What special benefits does your most used credit card provide?	
12. What is your opportunity cost of using credit cards?	

ACTIVITY 5

Name _____

Name of Institution	APR	Grace Period	Late Fees	Annual or Membership Fee	Cash Advance	Special Benefits

- Americans charged more than $350 billion on their bank credit cards in 1993.

- Americans paid $36 billion in credit card interest in 1993.

- The average credit cardholder has more than nine credit and charge cards.

- The typical cardholder who paid finance charges in 1993 spent nearly $460 in interest.

Source: *Financial Responsibility*, American Express, 1994.

VISUAL 2
BENEFITS OF CREDIT CARDS

- Earlier consumption; use of goods while paying for them

- Convenience

- Use for emergencies

- Establishment of a good credit history

- Consolidation of debts

- Identification

VISUAL 3
COSTS OF CREDIT CARDS

- Costs more if unpaid balance is not paid monthly

- Ties up future income

- Tempts one to overspend

- Reduces comparison shopping if you only shop in stores extending credit

- Decreases future buying power

VISUAL 4
THE 3 CS OF CREDIT

Capacity:
   Your ability to pay back a loan

Collateral:
   Your assets used as a guide to determine
   your ability to repay the debt

Character:
   Your reputation as a reliable and
   trustworthy person

LESSON 11
HOUSING: DECIDING TO RENT OR BUY

INTRODUCTION

We all require some form of shelter. This can be satisfied in a variety of ways. Among the alternatives are renting an apartment or purchasing a house or condominium. These options generally constitute a significant portion of our monthly budget. The median price of an existing home was $103,000 in 1993. Any major purchasing decision of this nature requires a reasoned approach to allocating our scarce economic resources. As with any market, buyers and sellers are guided by supply and demand to allocate goods and services. They must make informed choices in a changing economic environment. Thus, students should learn how to apply the decision-making model to purchasing housing services given their individual lifestyle.

CONCEPTS

Scarcity
Opportunity Cost
Interest
Market
Supply
Demand

CONTENT STANDARD

All decisions involve opportunity costs; weighing the costs and benefits associated with alternative choices constitutes effective economic decision making.

OBJECTIVES

◆ Identify alternative types of housing.

◆ Compare and contrast the advantages of different types of housing.

◆ Evaluate various housing alternatives based on relevant criteria by using a decision-making grid.

◆ Apply the decision-making process to a housing search.

◆ Investigate a potential housing purchase through a community-based research report.

LESSON DESCRIPTION

Students begin by learning to apply the decision-making process to a major purchasing decision, and they become acquainted with how to use a decision making grid. Next, students will participate in a simulation in which they are buyers and sellers of housing services. Some students will be buyers who must decide whether to rent or buy. Other students will be sellers who have houses or apartments to offer. Students must go to the marketplace to make their purchases.

TIME REQUIRED

Two or three class periods.

MATERIALS

Transparency of Visual 1
★ One copy for each student of Activity 1
One copy of the Seller Cards
One copy of the Buyer Cards
★ One copy for each student of Activity 2

PROCEDURE

DECISION GRID

1. Explain to students that the purpose of this lesson is to examine housing needs. Students will learn how to make effective purchasing decisions related to housing services and have a better understanding of the housing market.

2. Discuss how different family lifestyles affect the type of housing required. Point out that these housing desires change over time. Discuss how housing needs might differ among the following individuals and families:

a recent college graduate in an entry level professional job.

a young married couple with steady jobs

a married couple with 1 child approaching school age

a single parent with 2 children

a retired couple whose children are grown

3. Brainstorm different housing alternatives. The list will include rent an apartment or house; buy a house, mobile home, or condominium; build a house.

4. Display Visual 1, which identifies advantages of renting and buying. Discuss each advantage to be sure students understand each one. Refer to the discussion about lifestyles above.

5. Explain that decisions are not costless. *Scarcity* requires people to make choices about goods and services that will give the greatest satisfaction. For every choice, there is an opportunity cost. *Opportunity cost* is the highest valued alternative that must be forgone because another option is chosen.

6. Divide students into cooperative groups. Distribute Activity 1, and ask them to complete the decision-making grid using the PACED method outlined on the handout.

Step 1: Define the **P**roblem (to choose which type of housing is best)

Step 2: List your **A**lternatives (to rent or buy)

Step 3: State your **C**riteria (may include: mobility, tax advantages, transaction cost, investment potential, maintenance requirement, privacy or freedom, etc.)

Step 4: **E**valuate your alternatives. Use plus or minus signs in the appropriate box to indicate your assessment. (Answers may vary, although one suggested outcome is as follows:

Step 5: Make a **D**ecision: Frank and Sylvia should probably try to buy a home.

Have a student from each group present the group's decision grid. (You might want to make a transparency of Activity 1 to facilitate discussion.)

SIMULATION

1. Review the advantages of renting and buying if the simulation is conducted the next day. Explain to students that we make decisions about housing services in the marketplace in the same manner as we do for most of the goods and services we purchase. Tell students they will play a game in order to better understand the role of buyers and sellers in the housing market.

2. Designate 6 students to be sellers of housing services and 20 students to work in pairs as buyers (may be varied according to number of students in class by increasing the appropriate number of seller and buyer cards).

3. Give one housing card to each of the 6 sellers. They must develop advertisements for their property. Give one family card to each team of buyers. They must use the decision-making grid to make their purchasing decisions.

4. Allow students about 15 minutes to perform their respective tasks. The sellers should locate themselves around the classroom. Give students approximately 20 minutes to shop for housing services. When a buyer and a seller reach an agreement, they should put up a "sold" sign.

5. After the game is over, ask the students representing families to explain their decision to rent or to buy. Did all families agree to purchase

Alternatives	Criteria					
	Mobility	Tax advantage	Mortgage/ Rental Costs	Investment Potential	Low Maintenance	Privacy
Buy a house						
Rent apartment						

housing? If not, why? (Although there are corresponding buyer and seller cards, some students may make other choices. This can occur in any market.) Ask the following questions:

A. Were the sellers able to sell their housing services for the asking price? Did anyone agree on a lower price? Why?

B. What factors did the buyers consider? (income, number of children, lifestyle, etc.)

EXTENSION

Often people do not attempt to purchase a home because they believe it requires a much larger income and down payment than they have. Have students work on a research project in which they are given a certain level of income and must determine what type of housing and financing is feasible. A guest speaker from a real estate agency or a lending institution will help students complete a community-based survey. The survey will help students determine if they would qualify to purchase a home; and if so, what kind of home. Since each group will most likely contact different resource people in the community and the results may vary, it will have a more realistic outcome. Some may be told they do not qualify, others may discover there are special financing packages that assist first-time home buyers. The goal of this activity is to discover which group was able to obtain the most house for their level of income.

1. Divide class into cooperative groups of three or four students. Give students the following scenario:

You and your spouse have a combined monthly gross income of $2500. The only debt you have is a $200 monthly car payment and $50 each month on your credit card. Because you pay your bills on time, your credit rating is in good standing. For the past two years you have rented an apartment, and you are a first-time home buyer.

2. Instruct the students to use community resources to determine if they would qualify to purchase a home. They should search the newspaper classified ads, speak to a real estate agent, and check with a local bank. Activity 2 may be used as a guide for their interviews. Be sure they obtain a description of the type of house and the financing option.

3. Students should present their results to determine what type of housing may be purchased with this level of income. The information may be presented in a retrieval chart on the bulletin board, which will help students determine which group was able to meet their housing preferences most effectively.

4. This project may be used for writing or math portfolios. Students can write about their research experience and a thank you letter to the resource people who gave them information. Students might also discuss why an understanding of percentages and other calculations were important to this project.

VISUAL 1
HOUSING ALTERNATIVES

Advantages of Renting:

1. No down payment is needed; only a deposit is required.

2. Allows greater mobility if you decide to move again soon.

3. No maintenance costs and no responsibility of ownership.

4. Offers opportunity to become familiar with the community before you buy.

Advantages of Buying:

1. You plan to live in the same location.

2. There may be tax benefits.

3. May have investment potential and provide a type of forced savings.

4. Offers a feeling of independence and security.

ACTIVITY 1
PUTTING A ROOF OVER YOUR HEAD

Name _____

Frank and Sylvia met at the local technical college. They married shortly after graduation. They have a combined gross monthly income of $3500. Frank hopes to be promoted to a supervisory position within the company during the next five to 10 years. Sylvia would like to open her own business in a few years. One of their two cars is fully paid for. They have a $210 monthly payment on the other car. They have wedding gifts and savings totalling $5000.

Directions: Use the decision-making model to help Frank and Sylvia decide if they should rent an aprtment or buy a house.

> Step 1: Define the problem
> Step 2: List your alternatives (use the grid below)
> Step 3: State your criteria (use the grid below)
> Step 4: Evaluate your alternatives (use plus or minus signs in the appropriate box to indicate your assessment)
>
> Step 5: Make a decision

Alternatives	Criteria			

Explain why this choice is best for Frank and Sylvia.

SELLER CARDS

Instructions: Read the description of the type of housing you have to offer. Develop an advertisement for your home or apartment using the information you have been given. In a few moments you will have an opportunity to try to sell your housing services in the marketplace.

Seller #1: You are the builder of five new houses. Four other houses sold, and you want to sell this last house. It is located in one of the highest rated school districts in the area. Since this is the last house available, you are willing to negotiate the price. The following information may be helpful in developing your advertisement:

> *New home, 2 story*
> *4 bedroom, 2 ½ bath*
> *Excellent school district*
> *Family room with woodburning fireplace, large finished rec room, screened porch*
> *Price: $184,000*

Instructions: Read the description of the type of housing you have to offer. Develop an advertisement for your home or apartment using the information you have been given. In a few moments you will have an opportunity to try to sell your housing services in the marketplace.

Seller #2: Your employer has transferred you to its headquarters in another city. Six years ago you paid $112,000 for this house. The real estate broker will charge a 5% commission on the sale price of your home. The lowest offer you will accept is $123,000 ($116,850 after commission): The following information may be helpful in developing your advertisement:

> *Spacious, 4 bedroom, 2 ½ bath, w/all the extras*
> *Formal living room/dining room, 1st floor family room + laundry,*
> *basement, large porch*
> *Price: $129,900*

SELLER CARDS (CONTINUED)

Instructions: Read the description of the type of housing you have to offer. Develop an advertisement for your home or apartment using the information you have been given. In a few moments you will have an opportunity to try to sell your housing services in the marketplace.

Seller #3: You are a young married person whose first child is now six months old. The interest rates are favorable and you want to purchase a larger family home. Your purchase depends upon the sale of your existing home. This home is a good "starter home" for first-home buyers. Since you are selling the home yourself, you can anticipate $1,000 in fees to have a lawyer file the necessary paperwork. The lowest you will accept is $61,900. The following information may be helpful in developing your advertisement:

Brick, 2 bedroom, dining room, living room, fully equipped kitchen,
all amenities
For sale by owner
Price: $64,900

Instructions: Read the description of the type of housing you have to offer. Develop an advertisement for your home or apartment using the information you have been given. In a few moments you will have an opportunity to try to sell your housing services in the marketplace.

Seller #4: You are married with two children. You have decided to build a new home, and your real estate agent charges 6% commission on the selling price of the home. Ten years ago, you bought the house for $68,000. The following information may be helpful in developing your advertisement:

40-year old ranch, 3 bedroom, 2 bath
central air, garage, 1500 sq. ft.
Price: $75,000

SELLER CARDS (CONTINUED)

Instructions: Read the description of the type of housing you have to offer. Develop an advertisement for your home or apartment using the information you have been given. In a few moments you will have an opportunity to try to sell your housing services in the marketplace.

Seller #5: You are a young professional living in a condominium located in an urban neighborhood. Three years ago you paid $70,000 for this condominium. You recently married and want to move to a house in a more suburban area. The following information may be helpful in developing your advertisement:

> *2 bedroom, 2 bath*
> *equipped kitchen, laundry room, living room, dining room*
> *Patio w/storage*
> *Pool & clubhouse, tennis*
> *Price: $75,000*

Instructions: Read the description of the type of housing you have to offer. Develop an advertisement for your home or apartment using the information you have been given. In a few moments you will have an opportunity to try to sell your housing services in the marketplace.

Seller #6 - You are the manager of an apartment complex. It is your responsibility to rent apartments. Anyone wishing to rent an apartment must submit: (1) a $25 fee with the application, (2) a $250 deposit ($200 is refundable), and (3) one month's rent paid in advance. You do not allow pets. There are currently 5 apartments available. The following information may be helpful in developing your advertisement:

> *1 one bedroom at $400*
> *2 two bedroom/one bath at $485*
> *2 two bedroom/two bath at $500*
> *Large apartments. Clubhouse & fitness center, includes heat*
> *Access to interstate highway and close to university*

BUYER CARDS

Instructions: Read the description of your family situation. You must decide what type of housing would be best for you and your family. You may choose to rent an apartment, buy a house, or buy a condominium. The decision making grid will be a useful guide in making your choice. In a few moments you will have an opportunity to try to buy housing services in the marketplace.

Family A: Two-income family
Very stable employment
Combined gross annual income of $95,000
Bank has qualified you for up to $190,000
2 children, looking for housing in a good school system

Instructions: Read the description of your family situation. You must decide what type of housing would be best for you and your family. You may choose to rent an apartment, buy a house, or buy a condominium. The decision-making grid will be a useful guide in making your choice. In a few moments you will have an opportunity to try to buy housing services in the marketplace.

Family B: Two-income family
Combined gross annual income of $52,000
1 child

BUYER CARDS (CONTINUED)

Instructions: Read the description of your family situation. You must decide what type of housing would be best for you and your family. You may choose to rent an apartment, buy a house, or buy a condominium. The decision-making grid will be a useful guide in making your choice. In a few moments you will have an opportunity to try to buy housing services in the marketplace.

Family C: Two-income family
Recently married
Employed for two years in stable jobs
Own a Labrador Retriever dog
Enjoy the outdoors

Instructions: Read the description of your family situation. You must decide what type of housing would be best for you and your family. You may choose to rent an apartment, buy a house, or buy a condominium. The decision-making grid will be a useful guide in making your choice. In a few moments you will have an opportunity to try to buy housing services in the marketplace.

Family D: Single person
Professional career planning to remain in the area
Gross annual income $40,000

BUYER CARDS (CONTINUED)

Instructions: Read the description of your family situation. You must decide what type of housing would be best for you and your family. You may choose to rent an apartment, buy a house, or buy a condominium. The decision-making grid will be a useful guide in making your choice. In a few moments you will have an opportunity to try to buy housing services in the marketplace.

Family E: Retired couple
Receives gross Social Security and Retirement Pension of $4,000 per month
Recently sold a large old home and would like to downsize
Desire less maintenance and responsibility
Enjoy traveling

Instructions: Read the description of your family situation. You must decide what type of housing would be best for you and your family. You may choose to rent an apartment, buy a house, or buy a condominium. The decision-making grid will be a useful guide in making your choice. In a few moments you will have an opportunity to try to buy housing services in the marketplace.

Family F: Student
Gross monthly income of $1225
Attends the local university
Roommate pays half of rent and food expenses
Graduates in two years

BUYER CARDS (CONTINUED)

Instructions: Read the description of your family situation. You must decide what type of housing would be best for you and your family. You may choose to rent an apartment, buy a house, or buy a condominium. The decision-making grid will be a useful guide in making your choice. In a few moments you will have an opportunity to try to buy housing services in the marketplace.

Family G: Single adult
    Recently moved to the city to take a new job
    Gross annual income is $60,000
    Job requires weekly travel out of town by car
    Not familiar yet with the area

Instructions: Read the description of your family situation. You must decide what type of housing would be best for you and your family. You may choose to rent an apartment, buy a house, or buy a condominium. The decision-making grid will be a useful guide in making your choice. In a few moments you will have an opportunity to try to buy housing services in the marketplace.

Family H: Single parent
    Recently divorced with one child 10 years old
    Gross annual income is $28,000

BUYER CARDS (CONTINUED)

Instructions: Read the description of your family situation. You must decide what type of housing would be best for you and your family. You may choose to rent an apartment, buy a house, or buy a condominium. The decision-making grid will be a useful guide in making your choice. In a few moments you will have an opportunity to try to buy housing services in the marketplace.

Family I: Single adult
Recently moved to the city to take a new job
Gross annual income is $60,000
Job requires weekly travel out of town by car
Not familiar yet with the area

Instructions: Read the description of your family situation. You must decide what type of housing would be best for you and your family. You may choose to rent an apartment, buy a house, or buy a condominium. The decision-making grid will be a useful guide in making your choice. In a few moments you will have an opportunity to try to buy housing services in the marketplace.

Family J: Two-income family
Recently married
Gross annual income is $48,000
No savings accumulated

ACTIVITY 2
COMMUNITY-BASED SURVEY GUIDE

Name _____

Type of house:

a. What is the estimated purchase price?

b. How many rooms does the house have?

c. How many bedrooms?

d. How many bathrooms?

e. What is the size of the yard?

f. Describe the location.

Financing:

a. How much money might a bank be willing to lend at this income level?

b. What type and amount of down payment is required?

c. What is the interest rate?

d. What is the monthly payment?

e. What are the closing costs?

f. What other costs are included?

g. Describe special financing packages available for first-time home buyers.

Name of Resource Person

Company

LESSON 12 ADVERTISING: IS CONSUMER SOVEREIGNTY DEAD?

INTRODUCTION

High school students want a voice in the selection of the goods and services that they consume. They are much less likely to simply consume goods and services provided for them by their parents or other adults. In order to be good decision makers they need to learn how to gather and then evaluate information about the products they will be purchasing. A major source of information is advertising. By helping students become aware of the different types of advertising they will be able to make informed choices as they begin voting for products with their dollars.

CONCEPTS

Advertising
Consumer Sovereignty
Market System

CONTENT STANDARD

In a market economic system, the major decisions about production and distribution are made in a decentralized manner by individual households and business firms following their own self-interest.

OBJECTIVES

◆ State the purpose of advertising.

◆ Explain consumer sovereignty.

◆ Identify different types of advertising.

LESSON DESCRIPTION

Students are introduced to different types of advertising as well as the role advertising plays in a modern economy. They participate in a simulation that confronts the influence that advertising has on their behavior as consumers. Finally, they are asked to consider John Kenneth Galbraith's opinion on the degree of consumer sovereignty in the marketplace.

TIME REQUIRED

2 Days.

MATERIALS

Visual 1A, U.S. Advertising Expenditures 1930–1990 (in current dollars)
Visual 1B, U.S. Advertising Expenditures 1930–1990 (in constant 1990 dollars)
Visual 2, Advertising Techniques
★Activities 1 and 2
■Activity 3
Printed Advertisements (examples)
Card Stock for Puzzle Pieces
Three large bottles of cola: Coca-Cola, Pepsi-Cola, and a generic or local brand
18 small paper cups

PROCEDURE

DAY ONE

1. Begin with a general discussion of advertising. Include the fact that advertising expenditures in the United States have grown dramatically since the advent of television. (See Visual 1A.)

Year	Advertising Expenditures (billions of current dollars)
1930	3.4
1940	2.1
1950	6.0
1960	11.0
1970	19.0
1980	55.0
1990	120.0

2. An observant student might suggest that one 1930 dollar had more buying power than a 1990 dollar. Visual 1B adjusts these data for inflation and puts all expenditures in terms of 1990 buying power. As you can see, a 1930 dollar had about the same buying power as $8.50 in 1990. ($3.4 billion in advertising in 1930 was worth $29 billion in 1990 dollars).

Year	Advertising Expenditures (billions of 1990 dollars)
1930	29
1940	20
1950	31
1960	44
1970	56

★ all students–basic course material
■ average and above average students

1980	81
1990	120

Despite adjusting for inflation, you still see a dramatic rise in advertising expenditures. To put these data into a more personal perspective, you might divide the 1990 advertising expenditures by the number of households in the U.S. (approximately 93 million) to arrive at an expenditure of almost $1300 per household or approximately $480 per person in 1990. This compares to only $235 (in constant dollars) per person in 1930. The U.S. is spending twice as much on advertising today even after adjusting for inflation. Why is there so much more spending?

3. Write the term "Consumer Sovereignty" on the chalkboard. Briefly explain that this concept is critical to any market economy. Essentially consumer sovereignty is the belief that, in a market economy, it is the consumers who ultimately determine what goods and services are produced. Consumers "vote with their dollars." If there are enough dollar votes, then a product continues to be produced. Otherwise, firms must produce another product or go out of business.

4. Pose this question to the students for some general discussion:

Given these massive advertising expenditures, do you think consumer sovereignty is dead?

The discussion should be organized around some relevant examples. Most economists would argue that while consumer sovereignty is not evident in 100% of the U.S. economy, it is still very much alive. Some examples of the power of the American consumer are the prevalence of imported cars in the U.S.; the switch from the "New Coke" back to "Coke Classic" when consumers rebelled at the taste of New Coke; and the discontinuation of the IBM PC Jr. computer. Another famous example of consumer power was the Edsel automobile, which was introduced by Ford but never found a loyal following. Coca-Cola, IBM, and U.S. automakers would all prefer that consumers bought their products without question. But consumers do not always behave as producers would like.

5. Although consumers are the ultimate deci-sion makers, advertising can be an effective tool in reaching those decision makers. Question the class about the reasons businesses advertise. Some typical answers might be:
- to increase sales
- to provide information
- to develop and protect brand loyalty

6. Ask students how advertisers achieve these goals. Let students answer and then summarize by telling them that essentially there are three types of advertising:

A. Rational Appeal

B. Emotional Appeal

C. Testimonial Appeal

7. Run off enough puzzles, in different colors (card stock if possible), so that each student will be able to have one puzzle piece.

8. Place Visual 2 on the overhead projector and explain to students that they are going to be learning more about these different types of advertisements, which are used to market products. Briefly describe the characteristics of different types of advertising. (As background you might want to mention that rational appeal ads are often found in print media. Newspaper ads for local grocery stores where prices and brands are listed is an example of this type of advertising. Emotional appeal ads are often television or radio ads where the emphasis is on feeling good. The testimonial ads often have sports figures or other celebrities.)

9. Give each student a puzzle piece. Tell them to get up and find classmates who have the rest of the pieces of the puzzle. Then have groups put puzzles together and identify which type of advertisement the puzzle represents.

10. Once the students have formed their groups, give each group a copy of Activity 1. Have them identify what puzzle they have. Discuss the types of advertising as the students identify them. (You may want to project a transparency of the completed puzzle to help them see all the pieces as a whole.)

11. Have each group complete Activity 1. If time permits have them share their answers in a class discussion.

12. Give each student a copy of Activity 2, which they are to complete for homework. Tell them that you actually want them to watch some commercials on television with an eye for the kind of appeal that is being made. Ask them to consider if the ads they watch have a major influence on what they buy.

Day Two

13. Before you collect the homework assignment ask students for their impressions of the power of advertising on their behavior. Are the ads simply informational or are they persuasive? Have them give some examples and then collect their homework.

14. Now you are ready to try a consumer survey that will test the impact of advertising on their spending. Take a classroom survey of student preferences with regard to cola. Ask for a show of hands on how many prefer Coca-Cola? How many Pepsi-Cola? How many are indifferent? How many do not like any cola? Record the results on the board.

15. Get six volunteers—three from the Coke and three from the Pepsi groups—to come forward for the taste test. Have the volunteers face the wall while you pour each of them three cups of cola for the taste test. Have them sample Cola I, Cola II, and then Cola III. Have them each rank their preferences for the drinks.

16. Compare the results of the Taste Test among the three brands with their earlier preferences. Were they consistent? If not, ask them to explain the results in terms of advertising persuasion. If they were consistent, what does this mean in terms of consumer sovereignty?

CLOSURE

17. Give each student a copy of Activity 3, which contains some thoughts from John Kenneth Galbraith, a Harvard economist who has been an outspoken critic of the doctrine of consumer sovereignty. Have students read the passage, and then tell whether they agree with the "Accepted Sequence" (Consumer Sovereignty) or Galbraith's "Revised Sequence."

VISUAL 1A
U.S. ADVERTISING EXPENDITURES 1930–1990

Year	Advertising Expenditures (billions of nominal dollars)
1930	3.4
1940	2.1
1950	6.0
1960	11.0
1970	19.0
1980	55.0
1990	120.0

VISUAL 1B
U.S. ADVERTISING EXPENDITURES 1930–1990 (IN CONSTANT 1990 DOLLARS)

Year	Advertising Expenditures (billions of dollars)
1930	29
1940	20
1950	31
1960	44
1970	56
1980	81
1990	120

VISUAL 2
ADVERTISING TECHNIQUES

RATIONAL APPEAL:

◆ Reasonable Claims

◆ Logical Approach

◆ Basic Product and Price Information Provided

◆ Allows for Product Comparison

EMOTIONAL APPEAL:

◆ Aimed at Human Behavior

◆ Less than Reasonable Claims

◆ Emphasis on Feelings

◆ Little Product Information

TESTIMONIAL/CONFORMITY APPEAL:

◆ Very Little Product Information

◆ Often uses Celebrities

◆ Encouraged to be "Just Like Everyone Else"

◆ Use of Gimmicks

ACTIVITY 1

Name _____

Period _____

Names of Team Members

1.

2.

3.

4.

5.

The advertising type in our puzzle was

Real world examples of this type of advertising are the ads for:
(Write down all those your team can think of)

ACTIVITY 2

Name _____

Your assignment is to find examples of the following types of advertising techniques from newspapers, magazines, direct mail, radio, or television.

1. Rational Appeal

These ads are largely informative. Basic product information is presented in such a way as to invite price and product comparisons. Consumers have more information because of this ad. Newspapers and other print media are often good sources for these ads.

2. Emotional Appeal

These ads emphasize personal feelings. The results are very difficult to measure. They often make claims for the product but really give very little product information. They rely on emotions such as patriotism, maternal instinct, and the like.

3. Testimonial / Conformity Appeal

These ads often depend on the use of celebrities, but they could also be staged events where "real people" give their opinion. There is very little product information and the consumer is led to believe that using this good or service is a great idea because it is associated with the celebrity.

Advertisement	Type	Medium (TV, Magazine, etc.)

ACTIVITY 3
PROFESSOR GALBRAITH LECTURES ON CONSUMER SOVEREIGNTY *

Name _____

In virtually all economic analysis and instruction, the initiative is assumed to lie with the consumer. In response to wants that originate within himself.... The flow of instruction is in one direction—from the individual to the market to the producer. All this is affirmed, not inappropriately, by terminology that implies that all power lies with the consumer. This is called *consumer sovereignty*. There is always a presumption of consumer sovereignty in the market economy. The unidirectional flow of instruction from consumer to market to producer may be denoted the Accepted Sequence. [T]his sequence does not hold. The mature corporation has readily at hand means for controlling prices at which it sells as well as those at which it buys. Similarly, it has means for managing what the consumer buys at the prices which it controls....

The Accepted Sequence is no longer a description of the reality and is becoming ever less so. Instead the producing firm reaches forward to control its markets and on beyond to manage the market behavior and shape the social attitudes of those, ostensibly, that it serves. For this we also need a name and it may appropriately be called the Revised Sequence.

1. What is another term for the "Accepted Sequence"?

2. What does Galbraith mean by the "Revised Sequence"?

3. Which sequence is the more accurate description in the U.S. economy today? Did the Classroom Cola Challenge provide any support for these sequences?

---

* John Kenneth Gailbraith, *The New Industrial State*, 2nd Ed. (New York, Mentor Books, 1972), pp. 211–212.

PUZZLE PIECES 1/RATIONAL APPEAL

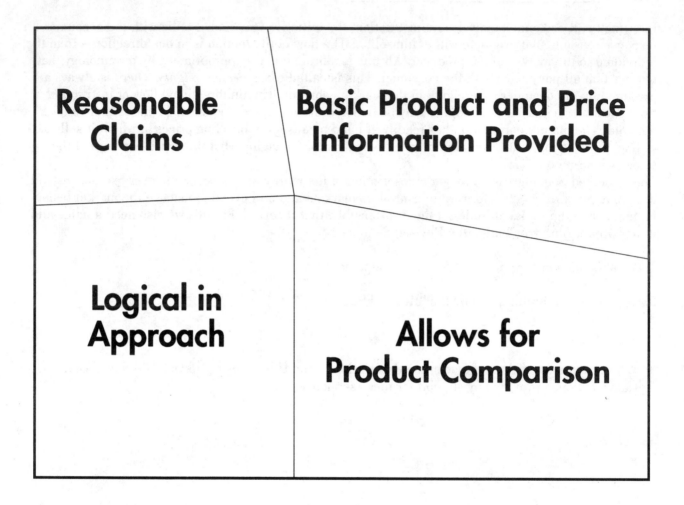

Reasonable Claims

Basic Product and Price Information Provided

Logical in Approach

Allows for Product Comparison

PUZZLE PIECES 2/EMOTIONAL APPEAL

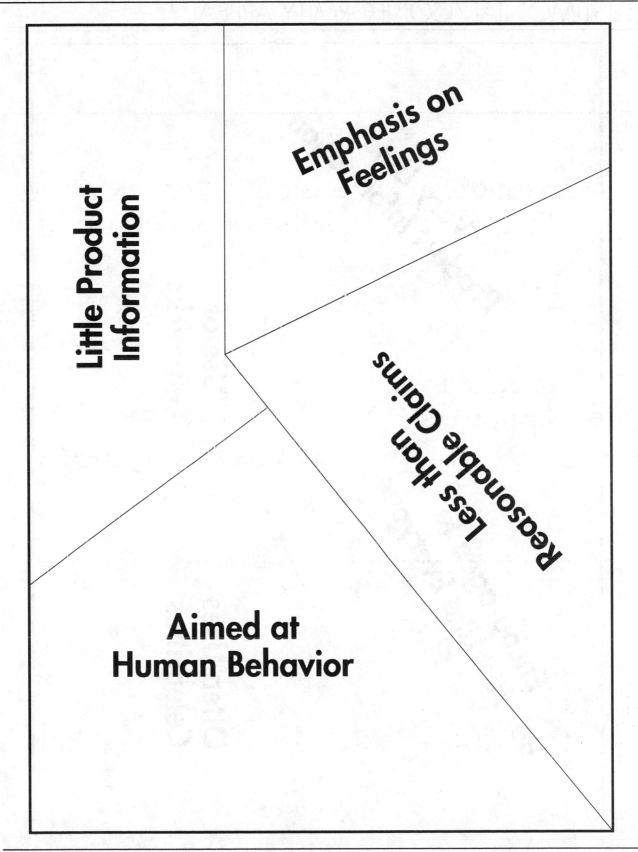

Little Product Information

Emphasis on Feelings

Less than Reasonable Claims

Aimed at Human Behavior

PUZZLE PIECES 3/
TESTIMONIAL/CONFORMITY APPEAL

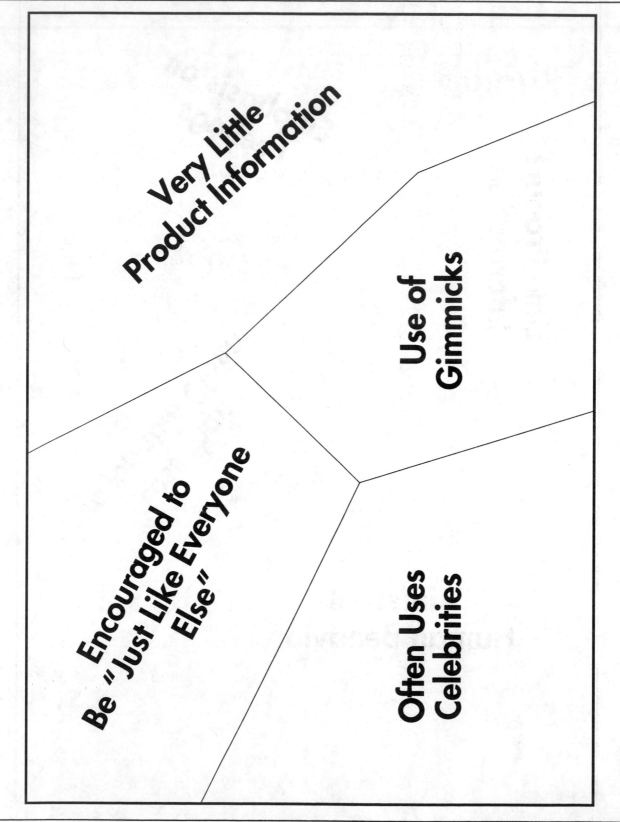

From *Personal Decision Making: Focus on Economics,* © National Council on Economic Education, New York, NY

LESSON 13
THE BASIC QUESTIONS OF HEALTH CARE: WHAT? WHY? HOW ?

INTRODUCTION

People in the United States are leading healthier lives and living longer than ever before. They are conscious of preventive care and are trying to practice good health habits. They also want quality and affordable health care. In 1993, Americans spent $850 billion or 14 percent of the country's total economic output on health care.

Health care is used by young and old alike; however, the elderly are the biggest users. They make up 10 percent of our population and use one-third of the health services. Health care includes various types of care that help keep us healthy, a state of complete physical, mental, and social well-being. Health care benefits include services from health care professionals, hospital expenses, surgical expenses, prescription drugs, vision care, and many others. Most health care expenditures are financed by third parties. Medicare, Medicaid, and private insurance companies are considered third parties. Basic health insurance guarantees certain health care services to the insured person for payment of a fixed sum each year. When purchasing a health care plan, you use the same decision-making process as you do when purchasing any good or service. First, state your problem. Second, analyze the costs and benefits of each option available. Then you make a decision. The PACED model can be used (See Lesson 2).

What is health care? Should I purchase health care? What kinds of coverage should I buy? This lesson focuses on these questions.

CONCEPTS
Choice
Opportunity cost
Demand
Decision making
Alternatives

CONTENT STANDARD

In a market economic system, the major decisions about production and distribution are made in a decentralized manner by individual households and business firms following their own self-interest.

OBJECTIVES

◆ Analyze the costs and benefits of health care plans.

◆ Apply the decision-making process to determine the purchase of health care plans.

LESSON DESCRIPTION

In a group activity, students use the decision-making process to analyze the costs and benefits of purchasing health care.

TIME REQUIRED
2 class periods.

MATERIALS
★ Copies of Activities 1, 1A, 2, 2B, 3, and 4
Transparency of Visual 1
Decision-making Grid (Optional)

PROCEDURE

1. Explain to students the focus of the lesson is health care. The lesson focuses on three questions: What is health care? Why do I need health care? How do I purchase health care to meet my needs?

2. Divide the class into two groups, A and B. To Group A, distribute Activities 1 and 1A. To Group B, distribute Activities 2 and 2B.

   A. Using a modified jigsaw puzzle method, divide Group A into smaller groups of 4 to 5 students. Do the same with Group B.

   B. Ask students to read the handout distributed to them, then discuss the questions assigned to their group.

★ all students–basic course material
■ average and above average students

3. Form new groups composed of three students from Group A and three students from Group B.

4. Each student will serve as an "expert" on their reading. Have "experts" from each team take turns explaining the major ideas from their reading.

(Alternate Activity: Distribute Activities 1 and 2 to students or groups of students. Discuss questions on Activities 1A and 2A with the whole group.)

5. In a whole group, explain to students there are many young and healthy people who for one reason or another do not have health care. They may be:

   A. *A college student who did not enroll in the college health plan*

   B. *A young man who has two part-time jobs*

   C. *A young professional who is between jobs*

   D. *An unemployed worker*

   E. *A new employee who failed to purchase health care during the open enrollment period*

   F. *A self-employed artist*

These are young and apparently healthy people. What unforeseen events may cause the individuals listed above to require doctors' care or short/long-term hospitalization. List possible situations. (Examples might include: skiing, surfing, or biking accidents, pregnancy, AIDS, leukemia, strep throat, pneumonia, diabetes, and cancer.)

5. Place Visual 1 on the overhead. Discuss the questions that should be considered before deciding on a health care plan.

6. If necessary, review the decision-making model with the students.

7 Have students get into groups. Distribute: (a) copies of three health plans, if available, or distribute (b) Activity 13-3. Assign each group an individual listed below. The task of each group is to study the health care needs of individuals listed below. Using a decision-making process, each group is to decide which plan provides the coverage needed and analyze the costs and benefits of each alternative. When each group completes Activity 3, ask them to share their decision-making process with the entire class.

   A. Jason is 21, married, and has one child. He works at a manufacturing plant. His employer pays part of his basic health care insurance that covers physician services, surgery, and hospital expenses. If Jason would like other benefits, he has to pay for them.

   B. Jennifer is 21 and single. To support herself while she is studying to be an actress, she has two part-time jobs. She wants to purchase health care and is investigating individual plans, their benefits, and cost.

   C. Kari recently graduated from college with a teaching degree. Her employer will contribute a set amount for health care insurance. She has a choice of three different health care plans. She will study each plan's costs and benefits before enrolling in a specific health plan.

   D. Michael just got married. He and his wife are artists and plan to spend a year traveling around the country looking for a place to settle. They want health care.

   E. David is single and a successful self-employed carpenter. He has just been diagnosed as a diabetic. His illness can be controlled with daily use of insulin.

OPTIONAL ACTIVITY

Explain that studies indicate your habits and your personal lifestyle can have a positive or negative effect on your health. This encourages the health care industry to promote wellness and fitness programs. Ask students: What is wellness? What are good health habits? Why does the health care industry promote wellness?

1. Distribute Activity 4, Wellness Survey to each student. After students complete their survey, have them assess their wellness rating by tallying the "Yes" responses.

Excellent, 10-12; Above Average, 8-9;
Average, 6-7;
Below Average, 4-5; Poor, below 4

2. Tally the range of responses. Have students or the teacher draw a bar or pie graph of the class wellness rating on the chalkboard. (*Optional:* have students give a wellness survey to their family members.)

ACTIVITY 1
HEALTH CARE

Name _____

People in the United States are leading healthier lives and are more conscientious about their health habits today than in years past. Health care has become a major economic issue. In 1993, Americans spent $850 billion or 14 percent of our country's total economy on health care. One out of every 20 people works in some area of health care, making it the third largest industry in the nation.

What is health care? It is care to insure your physical, mental, and social well-being. When you purchase health care, what are you buying? You purchase benefits and services from physicians, hospital expenses, surgical expenses, prescription drugs, vision care, substance abuse, and many other options. Most people do not pay directly for their health care expenses. They pay them through a third party, usually an insurance company or the government. Medicare, Medicaid, and a private insurance company such as Blue Cross/Blue Shield are considered third parties in health care.

As the cost of health care rises, the expense from long term illness, injury or disability can easily wipe out a family's savings or put them into debt. Health insurance reduces the risk of financial loss by having many individuals share the high cost of medical care by members of the group. It operates on the "share-the-risk" theory. Premiums from healthy, insured consumers help pay for those who become ill. Basic health insurance guarantees certain health services to the insured person for payment of a fixed sum each year. It protects the insured from financial loss for a relatively small fee. Health insurance is most commonly sold in a group plan that is cheaper than individual health plans. Group health plans are often fringe benefits provided by employers. Most employers offer some type of health insurance for full-time employees. Employers and employees usually share the cost of the premiums.

Many Americans do not have health insurance. It is estimated that nearly 37 million Americans lack insurance. There are many reasons for not having health insurance: it was not offered by their employers, they cannot afford to pay the insurance premiums (individual policies cost more than group rates) or they were dropped by their insurance company because of a certain illness or because of age.

Most family health plans provide coverage for children through age 18. What will you do when you are no longer covered by your parents' health insurance? Do you need health care when you are young and apparently healthy? What will you do after you are 19? Most universities and colleges offer low cost health plans to their students. However, the day you graduate, you are no longer covered.

Consumers want and demand more and better health care. Some factors that account for the rising demand for health care are (1) our growing aging population, (2) third party payments, and (3) new technology wanted by consumers. The elderly are the biggest users of health care. They make up 10 percent of our population and use one-third of the health services. Nearly 72% of health care costs are paid through a third party. When third parties pay for medical care, the quantity demanded for those services increases because there is no incentive for individual consumers or producers to be price conscious. Consumers also demand the use of the latest technology. For example, the high cost of obtaining an MRI (magnetic resonance imaging) scanner, or use of new and latest technology often add to the cost of health care.

From *Personal Decision Making: Focus on Economics*, © National Council on Economic Education, New York, NY

ACTIVITY 1A

Name _____

Discussion Sheet for Group A

Topic: What is health care?

Points to consider in your discussion:

• What do you purchase when you buy health care?

• How does health care insurance work?

• What are third party payments? How do they work?

• Who has health insurance? How did they get it?

• How many Americans don't have health insurance?

• How can you get health insurance?

• What conclusions about health care can you draw from the reading?

• What health care issues do you think you will face within the next few years?

ACTIVITY 2
CHALLENGES OF PURCHASING HEALTH CARE

Name _____

Purchasing health care is not an easy task. Unlike goods and services, purchasing health care is confusing because: (1) there are so many providers offering similar health services, (2) price information is not standardized and often difficult to obtain, and (3) it is difficult to select an insurance plan and supplemental plans that meet your health care needs and financial considerations. Health care decisions are often made in an emergency and the consumer does not have sufficient time to gather information. Decisions may be based upon reputation and confidence in the seller.

The biggest challenge in purchasing health care is comparing quality. When you buy a computer, stereo system, clothing, or a CD player, information about the products is available. It is easy to use the five-step decision-making model to help you decide which product to buy. You have some prior knowledge of the product or have received information from others that will help you evaluate the alternatives. It is not easy to use this same process when purchasing health care.

Comparing health care services is complex because most people do not have sufficient knowledge to judge the quality of services offered. Because health care needs are not the same for everyone, it is difficult to make comparisons. Another dilemma is price information. The cost of health care services is not easily available. Most physicians and hospitals do not publish their fee schedule. It is hard to find a list of the hospitals with the lowest room rates or lowest death rate and doctors with the lowest fees. Therefore, it is difficult for you to determine the quality of service from a fee schedule.

Selecting basic health insurance or supplemental plans to meet your health care needs and financial considerations is complex. Some of the vocabulary used may be unfamiliar, which adds to the confusion. To fully understand the benefits of various health insurance plans, you need an understanding of the effect of co-insurance, deductibles and exclusions have on the cost of your premium (cost of your insurance calculated on an annual, biannual, or monthly payment schedule). Co-insurance and deductible provisions generally lower the cost of your premium because you are sharing the cost of health care with the insurance company.

Co-insurance is an insurance plan in which part of the cost is shared by the insured person. For example, an insurance policy may pay 80 percent of the approved charges and the insured pays the remaining 20 percent of the cost.

Deductible is the initial dollar amount you must pay before the insurance begins paying.

Exclusions are the health care or related services that your insurance will *not* pay for.

In addition, when purchasing health care insurance, you need information about when you may enroll, change, or cancel your insurance plan. You also need to know the effective date of your insurance—what is the time period from when your premium is paid until your policy is in effect.

There are many types of health care insurance. To be a knowledgeable consumer, you need to understand the benefits, costs, and limitations of your coverage. You also need to analyze all the options, how they meet your health care needs and how you will pay for them. The basic categories in many plans are:

ACTIVITY 2 (CONTINUED)

Name _____

1. Basic coverage: ordinary hospital care, surgery, and physician services

2. Major medical: protection against the cost of serious or prolonged illness

3. Disability insurance: provides income for people who are unable to work because of sickness or injury

4. Dental insurance: provides coverage for the costs of dental services

5. Vision plan: provides coverage for eye exams, eyeglasses, and contact lenses

6. Prescription drug plan: copayment arrangement to obtain prescription drugs

7. Mental and substance abuse: provides coverage for psychiatric testing, inpatient and outpatient benefits

ACTIVITY 2B

Name _____

Discussion Sheet for Group B

Topic: Challenges of Purchasing Health Care

Points to consider in your discussion:

• Compare the differences between purchasing health care with other goods and services

• What kinds of coverage does health care insurance provide?

• What restrictions or policies do you need to know about when purchasing health care insurance?

• Compare the differences between purchasing health care and other goods and services.

• Describe a plan you would develop to investigate the various benefits provided by various health plans.

ACTIVITY 3
HEALTH INSURANCE COMPARISON CHART

Name _____

Benefits	Plan A	Plan B*	Plan C**
Physician Visits	80% EC of PP 70% EC of NP	$5 per visit	$5 per visit
Surgery	100% EC of PP 70% EC of NP	No charge	100% EC
Hospital	Pay contracted rate; pay difference between EC and charge; limit 150 days/yr	No charge Limit 365 days/yr	!00% EC
Hospice	100% EC Up to 150 days	No charge Up to 210 days	No charge Limit 180 days
Lab and X-Ray	100% EC of PP 70% EC of NP	No charge	Covered under physician and hospital benefits
Maternity	All physician and hospital benefits; no waiting period	No charge No waiting period	100% EC No waiting period
Mental Health and Substance Abuse	80% EC of PP 70% EC of NP 30 visits/yr	No charge Outpatient maximum 20 visits	75% of EC Outpatient $20 per visit
Ambulance	100% EC of PP 70% EC of NP	No charge	No charge
Vision	Not covered; can obtain vision plan	$5 per visit	Not covered; can obtain vision plan
Dental	Not covered; can obtain dental plan	Not covered; can obtain dental plan	Not covered; can obtain dental plan
Co-insurance/ Deductible	$1,000 - self $2,500 - family	$800 - self $2,400 - family	$1,250 - self $2,500 - family
Monthly Premium	Employee Employer $ 47.08 $70.60 $144.86 $217.30	Employee Employer $ 69.28 $70.60 $202.38 $217.30	Employee Employer $61.20 $70.60 $188.14 $217.30

- EC, Eligible charges
- PP, Participating provider
- NP, Nonparticipating provider

* Must attend specific clinic
** Must select physicians from approved list

ACTIVITY 4
DO I PRACTICE WELLNESS?

Name _____

Directions: Read each question carefully. Mark an **X** in the column that accurately describes your health habits.

YES	NO	WELLNESS QUESTIONS
		1. I exercise regularly (3 to 5 times per week).
		2. I get 7 to 8 hours of sleep nightly.
		3. I eat three balanced and nutritious meals per day that include the four food groups.
		4. I maintain proper weight control (not 10 pounds over suggested weight).
		5. I do not smoke cigarettes.
		6. I limit my intake of salt, sugar, and fats in my diet.
		7. I limit the intake of alcoholic beverages.
		8. I have been immunized for polio, small pox, mumps, rubella, tetanus, and diphtheria.
		9. I always wear a seatbelt when I drive or ride in an automobile.
		10. I try to learn about the health history of my family.
		11. I read about health issues regularly.

TOTAL NUMBER OF YES RESPONSES: _____

Excellent	10
Above average	8-9
Average	6-7
Below Average	4-5
Poor	0-3

My wellness rating is _____

What areas do I need to work on to improve my wellness rating? _____

VISUAL 1
GUIDELINES FOR PURCHASING SERVICES

1. Learn about the service you want to purchase

   • Research relevant facts and information

   • Get references from friends and workers in the field

2. Check for registration, certification and licensure

   • Look for indicators of a person's qualifications to provide quality services

3. Identify consumer problems related to the service you want to purchase

   • Seek out and use a variety of sources to identify problems unique to a particular service

4. Inquire about complaint procedures

5. Develop a short list of criteria that are most important to you

LESSON 14
SAVINGS AND PERSONAL INVESTMENTS: IF YOU'RE SO SMART, WHY AREN'T YOU RICH?

INTRODUCTION

Deciding how to save or invest money is important and exciting. But because there are many different saving and investment possibilities, understanding and evaluating the options can be confusing. The purpose of this lesson is to introduce students to some basic saving and investment options and vocabulary. Students apply The Decision Grid introduced in Lesson 2 to evaluate the trade-offs involved in five different saving or investment opportunities.

CONCEPTS

Capital
Investment
Savings
Opportunity cost
Securities: stocks, bonds, mutual funds
Savings accounts, certificates of deposit
Risk versus return
Liquidity

CONTENT STANDARD

In every economic system, consumers, producers, workers, savers, and investors seek to allocate their scarce resources to obtain the highest possible return, subject to the institutional constraints of their society.

OBJECTIVES

◆ Review and discuss different meanings for the terms "investment" and "capital."

◆ Discuss basic rules for wise investing.

◆ Demonstrate understanding of five different investment options using a decision grid.

LESSON DESCRIPTION

Students view a transparency showing the difference between economics definitions and personal finance definitions of the terms *capital* and *investment*. They read and discuss a handout listing four basic rules for wise investment decisions. In groups of five, they learn about different options for saving or investing money. They evaluate the different investment alternatives using The Decision Grid from Lesson 2. (It is not necessary to complete Lesson 2 before this activity, although you may wish to do so.)

TIME REQUIRED

One to two class periods.

MATERIALS

Overhead transparency of Visual 1
★ One copy of Activity 1 and Activity 2 for each student

PROCEDURE

The content of this lesson is appropriate for lower-achieving students. However, you may wish to simplify some of the vocabulary.

1. Announce to the class that they will take part in an activity to learn about different ways to save and invest wisely. Display Visual 1 to the class. Read through the definitions with students. Discuss how the personal finance definitions of *capital* and *investment* differ from the economics definitions. Tell students that in this lesson, *investment* will be used in the personal finance sense.

Define *savings* as refraining from consuming (after paying taxes). Discuss this idea in terms of the opportunity cost of saving: when people save, they give up current consumption.

Ask students why people save, since they are giving up the opportunity to consume now. List the reasons on the board. Make sure that students bring out the idea that people save in order to meet future needs.

You may wish to discuss some different ways to save and invest (e.g. savings accounts, stocks, bonds) at this point as an introduction to later parts of the lesson.

2. Distribute a copy of Activity 1 to each student. Discuss the investment advice with students. Add any further advice for sound investing to the list that you wish. The *Rule of 72* is introduced as an interesting way for students to see that different interest rates can make a big difference in long-run returns. However, people need to be aware of investment scams and fraud, and should be suspicious of schemes which promise very high returns.

3. Divide the class into groups of five students. Distribute a copy of Activity 2 to each student. (Or, you may wish to cut this handout into sections and give each student one part to play. This may promote more discussion within the group.) Read the introductory paragraph with the class. Have each student assume the role of one of David's relatives who offers him investment advice. Give students a few minutes to practice their part, then have students read their parts to their group.

4. With the class as a whole, discuss some advantages and disadvantages of the different investment options. After a few minutes, point out that a good way to evaluate the options would be to use a decision grid. (You may wish to see Lesson 2 before conducting this activity.) Read through the instructions for completing the decision grid with students. For students unfamiliar with using decision grids, it may help to make a grid on the board or overhead and complete the grid with the class as a whole. Students familiar with decision grids may complete the grid in their groups.

Possible criteria include liquidity (ease of converting into cash), ease of opening the account or making the investment, and ease of understanding the investment. The safety of the investment (lack of risk) is another important criterion. You may wish to supplement the information in Activity 2 to cover these criteria in more detail.

Ask all students to write an answer to the ques-

tion at the bottom of Activity 2, and ask students to give reasons for their choices.

5. Ask each group to summarize their decision grids to the class. The criteria identified by the groups and the evaluations are likely to vary. What would the groups decide, if they were in David's place? Point out to students that there is no one correct decision for David; his choice depends on his goals and priorities. Remind students that they should think for themselves and seek additional information before they act on any investment advice, even from relatives.

CLOSURE

There are many ways to expand this activity. Students could expand Activity 2 by researching and writing up other investment options. They could report on common investment fraud schemes, or the prospect of "investing" in a lottery. You could offer students a "what if" situation by asking them to assume that they had invested $1,000 twenty years ago. Have them research how various investments fared over the past twenty years.

VISUAL 1
ECONOMICS DEFINITIONS

INVESTMENT: spending by businesses on capital goods such as factories, tools, and machinery.

Sometimes called "real investment." Investment in this sense results in capital formation and leads to economic growth.

CAPITAL: goods produced by people to help them make other goods.

Sometimes called "capital goods" or "real capital." The economic definition of capital refers to things such as factories, machines, and tools.

PERSONAL FINANCE DEFINITIONS

INVESTMENT: buying assets such as stocks or bonds with the expectation of earning interest or income, or making a profit.

CAPITAL: an asset such as money owned or used by a person or a business.

Using personal finance definitions, capital is used to invest in something to try to produce more money or wealth for the investor.

ACTIVITY 1
SOME INVESTMENT ADVICE

Name _____

1. *Shop around for the best places to invest.*

   – look for low fees
   – look for high rates of return

   Rule of 72: To estimate how many years it will take a certain amount of money left in a compound-interest bearing account to double, take the interest rate and divide it into 72. It takes about 24 years for your savings to double if it grows at 3%, because 72 divided by 3 = 24.

   For example: $100 in an account that pays 2% will increase to $200 in about 36 years.
   $100 in an account that pays 4% will increase to $200 in about 18 years.
   $100 in an account that pays 8% will increase to $200 in about 9 years.

2. *Avoid investment scams. If it sounds too good to be true, it probably is!*

   People who promise very high rates of return and who contact you over the phone, by mail, on the street, or by going door to door are likely to be part of shaky or fraudulent schemes that are not worth your time and money. Often these people are very convincing salespeople; they have to be, since they earn their living by deceiving people.

   Put your savings into established financial institutions such as banks, savings and loans, or credit unions. Deal with reputable brokerage firms or trustworthy financial advisers.

3. *Carefully assess your saving and investment goals.*

   How much money do you have to save or invest?

   How much risk are you willing to take?

   How much liquidity (access to your money) do you require?

4. *Learn about different types of bank accounts and investment opportunities.*

   How safe are they? What are the rates of return? How easy is it to get your money out?

   Don't be afraid to ask questions of bankers and brokers. It's your money, so make sure you understand what you're doing!

ACTIVITY 2
WHERE TO INVEST $1,000

Name _____

David Rodriguez, a high school junior, has just inherited $1,000 from a distant relative. Although David would like to spend the money now, he has decided to put it away for college. At a family gathering, five of his relatives offer David the following advice about the best way to save or invest his money. (Please note that the analysis for the following scenarios ignores the possibility of loss of purchasing power due to inflation.)

AUNT ANDREA: David, I highly recommend that you invest your money in the **stock market.** When you buy a stock, you are buying ownership in a corporation. You earn money if the stock pays a dividend, or if you sell the stock for more than you paid for it. Of course, investing in stocks can be risky and you could lose money in the stock market too. (*Risk* refers to how likely you are to gain or lose money.) When you sell the stock, if its price has fallen below what you paid for it, you would lose part of your $1,000. If the stock becomes totally worthless, you would lose your whole $1,000. Whether you gain or lose depends on how well your stocks perform, which depends to a large extent on how well the company is doing. According to *The Wall Street Journal*, since 1926 your chances of losing money in the stock market in any one year are about 30%. However, over a ten year period, your chances of losing money are only about 4%! This means that the vast majority of people who purchase stocks as a long-term investment gain, and some gain a lot. Because there are so many different stocks to choose from (over 34,000), I suggest that you consult with a reputable stockbroker to help you decide how to invest your $1,000 in stocks. In general, you have to go through a stockbroker in order to buy or sell shares of stock, and you have to pay a commission to the broker. Your broker can tell you how your stock is doing, or you can keep track of its progress through the stock market pages in the daily newspaper.

SISTER SARA: David, I think you should keep your money in a traditional savings account at our local bank. These are often called "passbook accounts" because the bank will give you a small book to record your deposits and withdrawals. I know that **passbook savings accounts** generally earn lower interest than other types of savings accounts or other types of investments. But these accounts have advantages, too. For one thing, there is virtually no risk of losing any of your money because these accounts are insured by the FDIC for up to $100,000. Also, you can withdraw your money any time you want to without an interest penalty. It is really easy to open a passbook savings account, and easy to keep track of what's going on in your account.

UNCLE ALLEN: David, my suggestion is that you invest in a good **mutual fund**. A mutual fund company will pool your money together with that of thousands of other investors and buy many different *securities* (stocks and/or bonds). That way, if one stock or bond in the fund does poorly, the loss can be balanced by gains of other stocks or bonds in the fund. This allows you to *diversify* (distribute your investment among different types of securities to minimize risk). Mutual funds are managed by professionals who research what securities should go into the funds. Why not let experts make decisions for you? Of course, you have some decisions to make. You have to decide which fund you want to buy into, and there are over 3,000 funds to chose from. You can limit your choices by deciding if you want a very safe mutual fund or if you're willing to take more risk. Investors usually earn more profit from the riskier funds, but some people do not want to take the risk of losing their money. An example of a mutual fund that is usually relatively safe would be one that invests mainly in U.S. government bonds. A risky fund might invest in stocks of new companies that stand to either win big or lose big. And there are lots of choices in between. Although there is no guarantee of making a profit, in

ACTIVITY 2 (CONTINUED)

Name

general mutual funds have strong payout and safety records, especially for long-term investors. You may purchase mutual funds and learn about them through reputable brokers or financial planners, and you would have to pay them a commission for their services. If you do your own research and decide what fund you want to buy, you may usually call the fund directly and avoid the commission charge. You will receive statements that tell you how your mutual fund is doing, or you can read the tables in the newspaper.

GRANDMA BETTY: David, I think you should consider investing in **bonds**. A bond is like an I.O.U. For example, if you bought a municipal bond with your $1,000, you would be lending a state or local government $1,000. You could also buy a corporate bond or a U.S. government bond. You would earn a specified amount of interest on your bond while you own it. You could either keep the bond until it matures, at which time you would be paid back your $1,000, or you could sell the bond to another investor whenever you want. The price for which you would sell the bond would be determined by supply and demand in the bond market, and is related to interest rates on similar bonds. In other words, if you bought a $1,000 bond that matured in 10 years but you wanted to sell it in five years, you might sell it for more or less than $1,000. Some bonds work a little differently: you would pay less than $1,000 for them, and receive $1,000 when they mature. The difference between the purchase price and the maturity price would reflect the interest you have earned. As with other types of investments, in general, the safer the bond, the lower the rate of return. For example, a new company may promise very high rates of return on a $1,000 corporate bond, but if the company fails they would not be able to pay back the $1,000. U.S. government bonds are a very safe investment, but have relatively low rates of return. It's easy to buy some types of bonds. U.S. Savings Bonds can be purchased at your local bank . People who live close to a Federal Reserve Bank can buy U.S. Treasury

bonds there without paying any commission fees. Treasury bonds may also be purchased by mail from the Federal Reserve Bank of New York. In many cases, people buy bonds through brokers and pay a commission for the broker's services.

BROTHER TOM: David, in my opinion you should look into putting your $1,000 into a CD. No, no, not a compact disk! I mean a **certificate of deposit**. You have to have at least $500 to buy a CD, but that's no problem for you since you have $1,000. You earn higher interest than you would in other types of bank accounts. CDs are easy to buy; you just have to make a deposit into a CD account at almost any bank. When you make the deposit, you agree to leave the money in the account for a certain amount of time, usually between one month and five years. Generally, the longer you leave your money in, the higher the interest. However, if you withdraw your money early, you lose a lot of the interest. Also, if interest rates go up and you're locked into a long-term CD, you may wish you could switch your money into a different account. You have virtually no risk of losing your money, because your investment would be insured up to $100,000. There are no commission charges if you buy the CD at a bank.

ACTIVITY 2 (CONTINUED)

Name _____

Decision-Making Grid: What Should David Do?

Using a Decision-Making Grid like the one below could help David decide what to do with his $1,000.

1. Fill in the options (alternatives) David is considering in the first column. (The first one has been done for you.)

2. *Criteria* refers to the goals that David may consider to be important. What things might David consider in making his decision? One idea has been filled in for you. Fill in other possible criteria in the other columns.

3. Next evaluate the criteria for the different alternatives, using pluses and minuses. For example, a **+** has been placed in the row next to stocks under the criterion "possible high rate of return," because stocks meet this criterion well.

Alternatives for David's $1,000	**CRITERIA (Goals)**			
	Possible high rate of return			
Stocks	**+**			

If you were David, what would you do with your $1,000, and why?
(Write your answer here.)

LESSON 15
INTERNATIONAL ECONOMICS: WHY SHOULD YOU CARE?

INTRODUCTION

News broadcasts frequently mention items pertaining to international economics: free trade agreements such as NAFTA, trade deficits, and exchange rates. Students may believe, and rightly so, that analysis of these events can be very complicated. But international economics often directly affects American consumers. The purpose of this lesson is to introduce students to some of the ways in which they are affected by international economics, and to attempt to de-mystify some of the concepts.

CONCEPTS

Exchange rates
Effects of currency depreciation on consumers
Imports
Exports
Tariffs
Winners and losers from restrictions on trade

CONTENT STANDARD

Increasingly, we live in a global economy where what is done in this nation affects the rest of the world, and what is done there affects this nation. Economic issues associated with this trend must be analyzed by examining trends in trading levels, investments, foreign exchange values, and changes in public policies affecting these sectors.

OBJECTIVES

◆ Interpret an exchange rate table from a newspaper and recognize that exchange rates may fluctuate frequently.

◆ Identify ways in which currency depreciation and appreciation may affect consumers, investors, and travelers.

◆ Evaluate the effects of a protective tariff on people who may be directly or indirectly affected by the tariff.

LESSON DESCRIPTION

Students study an exchange rate table found in a local newspaper, and answer questions about exchange rates and their fluctuation. They read a short article on how a depreciation of the dollar could affect American consumers, and answer questions extending this concept. Students participate in a group activity where they analyze effects of a restrictive tariff on different groups of Americans, and draw conclusions about winners and losers from restrictions on free trade.

TIME REQUIRED

Two or more class periods, depending on the depth in which concepts are covered.

MATERIALS

■ One copy for each student of Activities 1, 2, and 3.

PROCEDURE

The content of this lesson is appropriate for high-achieving students and average-ability students. Some low-achieving students could complete the activities with extended assistance.

1. Tell students that they are going to learn about some of the aspects of international economics that affect them. If possible, bring in a recent newspaper article or refer to a recent news broadcast about the value of the dollar in foreign exchange markets. Discuss the news item with the class. Ask students to give reasons why Americans may want foreign currency, or why foreigners may want American dollars. (Major reasons include that Americans need foreign currency when they travel abroad, if they import foreign goods, or if they wish to invest in foreign securities. Foreigners need American dollars if they travel in the U.S., if they import U.S. goods, or if they wish to invest in U.S. securities. Some students may know that some people hold foreign currency for speculative purposes.) Pass out a copy of Activity 1 to each student, and ask them to choose a partner with whom to work. Have each student complete the questions on Activity 1, verifying their answers with their partner.

2. Discuss the answers to Activity 1 with the class. (1. 237.8; 239.4. 2. Answers will vary. 3.

★ all students–basic course material
■ average and above average students

1.47; 1.47. 4. Answers will vary. 5. The dollar would have bought more pounds on Monday than on Friday; therefore it would have been better for an American to exchange dollars for pounds on Monday.)

3. Pass out a copy of Activity 2 to each student. Still working in pairs, ask students to read the article and answer the questions that follow. When students have finished, discuss the answers with the class as a whole. (1. When the dollar falls against the pound, British goods will become more expensive for Americans. It will be more expensive for American tourists to travel in Britain. British securities would be more expensive to American investors. 2. If the dollar rose against the peso, Mexican goods and services, securities, and travel in Mexico would be cheaper for Americans. 3. If one American dollar buys 1.1 Canadian dollars, it would take $454.55 to buy 500 Canadian dollars. If one American dollar buys 1.5 Canadian dollars, it would take $333.33 to buy 500 Canadian dollars.)

Define *imports* and *exports* with students. Ask students to suggest reasons why countries trade with other countries. Write the suggestions on the board. Tell students that the purpose of the next activity is to consider who wins and who loses from free trade and from restrictions on free trade. Ask each pair of students to combine with another pair so that now there are four students in each group. Pass out a copy of Activity 3 to each student, and read the introductory paragraphs with the class. Ask each group to discuss how the people mentioned on the handout would be affected by the protective tariff on cars. Have all students write the group ideas on the handout.

5. Next have one person in each group assume the role of the U.S. auto worker, another that of the U.S. car buyer, another the California farmer who exports the products, and the fourth the worker in the imported car dealership. Ask all the auto workers to form one group, the consumers another group, the exporting farmers another, and the import car dealers another, so that there are four groups. Combining ideas from the prior groups, ask each new group to prepare a written statement representing their position on the protective tariff. (For example, the group containing

U.S. auto workers will write a statement stating and explaining whether they are for or against the tariff on foreign cars and why. The consumers will do the same, etc.) Have a spokesperson from each group read the statements to the class. Summarize the major points on the board. Statements may include the following points:

U.S. auto workers: would probably benefit from the tariff, which makes the price of foreign cars more expensive. Since U.S. cars become relatively less expensive, more U.S. cars would be sold, all other things remaining the same. This may make the workers' jobs more secure, or may result in pay raises for them.

Car consumers: would probably be hurt by the tariff, since it raises the price of foreign cars. In general, consumers benefit by competition because they may choose from more and better products at lower prices, and tariffs restrict competition. Even if the consumer planned on buying a U.S. car, the tariff could hurt them because domestic car companies would not have as much incentive to keep prices down and quality up to compete with foreign producers.

Farmers producing goods for export: would probably not benefit by a protective tariff on another product. Other countries may retaliate by putting tariffs on imports into their countries, which may restrict the amount of goods the farmers could sell abroad. Also, imports generate exports. If the U.S. imports cars, dollars are provided in foreign exchange markets that may be used to purchase U.S. exports, such as agricultural goods.

A salesperson working for an imported car dealership: would probably not benefit from the tariff. The prices of the products he or she sells would be higher, so people would not buy as many cars from the dealership. Many other workers dealing with exports and imports, and stockholders in the companies involved, could also be affected.

6. Next ask students to think about *long-run* effects of restrictive trade policies. If the U.S. and other countries regularly used trade restrictions to protect uncompetitive industries, what would happen to world output ten years from now? (Output

would be lower because the inefficient industries that benefit from trade restrictions could not produce as much as highly competitive industries.) What would happen to world consumption levels? (There would not be as many goods and services for people to consume.)

7. To summarize this activity, make a list on the board of some "winners" and "losers" from *free-trade policies*. Point out to students that people who benefit from trade restrictions are generally small in number and are often in specific industries that cannot compete effectively with foreign businesses. Free trade brings about benefits to consumers who may wish to buy imported goods, and may also benefit people in the U.S. whose jobs involve imports and exports.

CLOSURE

The table in Activity 1 could easily be updated using a recent newspaper. The activities in this lesson could serve as an introduction to a discussion of more complex issues involving international finance, balance of payments accounts, and the law of comparative advantage.

ACTIVITY 1
FOREIGN EXCHANGE RATES

Name _____

Newspapers publish a table like the one below to show how many dollars it takes to purchase one unit of a foreign currency (columns 2 and 3 below), or to show how much foreign currency it takes to purchase one dollar (the last two columns below). To purchase one British pound, for example, you would pay a little more than $1.53 as shown in column 2, or you could say that it would take about two-thirds of a pound (.65) to buy one U.S. dollar on Monday, July 25, 1994 (look at column 4 to check this). After looking at the table, answer the questions that follow.

Country (currency)	Foreign Currency in Dollars (Monday)	Foreign Currency in Dollars (Friday)	Dollar in Foreign Currency (Monday)	Dollar in Foreign Currency (Friday)
Argentina (Peso)	1.0100	1.0100	.9901	.9901
Australia (Dollar)	.7377	.7377	1.3556	1.3556
Austria (Schilling)	.0903	.0896	11.070	11.160
Belgium (Franc)	.0309	.0305	32.39	32.77
Brazil (Real)	1.0638	1.0638	.9400	.9400
Britain (Pound)	1.5382	1.55420	.6501	.6434
Canada (Dollar)	.7203	.7211	1.3883	1.3867
Chile (Peso)	.002427	.002427	411.99	411.99
China (Yuan)	.1125	.1125	8.8889	8.8889
Colombia (Peso)	.001225	.001225	816.00	816.00
France (Franc)	.1859	.1846	5.3800	5.4170
Germany (Mark)	.6355	.6303	1.5735	1.5865
Greece (Drachma)	.004205	.004177	237.80	239.40
Hong Kong (Dollar)	.1294	.1294	7.7250	7.7250
India (Rupee)	.0321	.0321	31.130	31.130
Indonesia (Rupiah)	.000461	.000461	2168.02	2168.02
Ireland (Punt)	1.5262	1.5163	.6552	.6595
Israel (Shekel)	.3298	.3298	3.0320	3.0320
Italy (Lira)	.000633	.000628	1579.00	1592.00
Japan (Yen)	.010101	.009990	99.00	100.10
Jordan (Dinar)	1.4704	1.4704	.68009	.68009
Malaysia (Ringgit)	.3855	.3854	2.5938	2.5950
Mexico (Peso)	.294421	.294507	3.3965	3.3955
Portugal (Escudo)	.006250	.006180	160.00	161.82
Russia (Ruble)	.000487	.000487	2052.00	2052.00
Saudi Arabia (Riyal)	.2667	.2666	3.7500	3.7507
Singapore (Dollar)	.6619	.6618	1.5107	1.5111
Spain (Peseta)	.007673	.007626	130.33	131.13
Sweden (Krona)	.1292	.1289	7.7415	7.7570
Switzerland (Franc)	.7539	.7438	1.3265	1.3445
Uruguay (Peso)	.200000	.200000	5.00	5.00

From *Personal Decision Making: Focus on Economics,* © National Council on Economic Education, New York, NY

ACTIVITY 1 (CONTINUED)

Name_____

1. Look at the last two columns in the table. On Monday, how many Greek drachmas could be purchased with one dollar?

   On Friday, how many Greek drachmas could be purchased with one dollar?

2. List three foreign currencies (other than the Greek drachma) whose value in terms of dollars changed between Monday and Friday.

3. Look at columns 2 and 3 in the table. On Monday, how many dollars could be purchased with one dinar from Jordan?

   On Friday, how many Jordanian dinars could be purchased with one dollar?

4. List three foreign currencies (other than the Jordanian dinar) whose value remained stable between Monday and Friday.

5. Say that you are planning a trip to Britain, and needed to trade dollars for British pounds. Would you have been better off to do this on Monday or on Friday? Explain.

ACTIVITY 2
THE CHANGING VALUE OF THE DOLLAR AND YOU

Name _____

From the exchange rate table on Activity 1, you saw that the value of the dollar in terms of foreign currency often fluctuates. Why might this be important to you? Read the following article and answer the questions that follow.

What the Dollar's Rise or Fall Means to You

News broadcasts and newspaper headlines often bombard you with announcements such as "The Value of the Dollar Rises in International Trading" or "The Dollar Reaches All-time Low Against the Japanese Yen" or "The Dollar Rallies." What does this mean to an average American consumer?

If you buy a Sony Walkman, somewhere along the way American dollars must be exchanged for Japanese yen. The people in Japan who produced the Walkman want to be paid in yen, not dollars. Although you personally do not have to go to the bank to exchange the dollars for yen and send the yen to Japan, someone else needs to do the equivalent of this in order for you to buy a product imported from Japan. In the same way, if you are traveling to a foreign country or if you want to invest in foreign stocks or bonds, dollars need to be exchanged for foreign currency.

If the dollar depreciates or falls, it means that the dollar does not buy as much foreign money as it did before. To see how this could affect consumers, let's look at the Walkman example again. In 1985, one dollar could be exchanged for 260 Japanese yen. In 1994, one dollar could be exchanged for 100 yen. Assume that the price of the Walkman was 10,000 yen and did not change between 1985 and 1994. How much would the Walkman cost an American consumer?

In 1985: 10,000/260 = $38.46 for a Walkman

In 1994: 10,000/100 = $100.00 for a Walkman

Because the dollar depreciated against the yen, Japanese goods became more expensive for Americans. When the dollar depreciates against the yen, it also becomes more expensive for American tourists to travel in Japan, and for American investors to purchase Japanese stocks or bonds. At the same time, all other things remaining the same, American products would become cheaper for Japanese consumers and investors, and travel in the U.S. would be cheaper for Japanese tourists.

Why does the value of the dollar rise and fall with respect to foreign money? In large part due to supply and demand. For example, American consumers supply dollars on foreign exchange markets to buy foreign products, and foreign consumers demand American dollars to buy American products. If the supply of dollars is greater than the demand for dollars at a certain exchange rate, the value of the dollar falls. In addition to forces of supply and demand, sometimes central banks intervene in the currency market to try to control the value of the dollar or other currencies. For example, they might buy U.S. dollars to make them scarcer and thus raise the value of the dollar in relation to other currencies. To lower the value of the U.S. dollar they would sell dollars in the international money markets, thus increasing their supply in those markets.

ACTIVITY 2 (CONTINUED)

Name _____

1. If the dollar falls in value against the British pound, how might this affect American consumers, investors, and travelers?

2. The examples in the article referred to a fall in the value of the dollar. Say that you heard on the news that the value of the dollar rose (or the dollar appreciated) against the Mexican peso. How might this affect American consumers, investors, or travelers? Explain.

3. Say that you hope to travel to Quebec with your school's French club. The trip is estimated to cost you $500 in Canadian dollars. Figure the cost to you in American dollars if the exchange rate is:

   1 American dollar = 1.1 Canadian dollars _____

   1 American dollar = 1.5 Canadian dollars _____

ACTIVITY 3
TRADE POLICIES: WHO WINS AND WHO LOSES?

Name _____

Governments may impose several types of policies that either encourage or discourage free trade between nations. For example, they may impose or reduce tariffs and quotas, or they may sign or fail to sign free trade agreements. In each case, some people win and some people lose from the policy. Complete the following exercise to help you to identify some of the winners and losers from a hypothetical example involving a tariff, a tax on imports.

Say that the United States is considering imposing a tariff on cars imported into the United States from foreign countries. This tariff would result in raising the price on all imported cars by $500.00. For each of the following groups of people, identify whether you think they would benefit from this tariff or not, and give reasons for your answer.

A. Workers living in Detroit employed by a United States auto manufacturer, making cars that are sold primarily in the United States.

B. Young couples and other consumers in the United States saving to buy a new car. They have been comparison shopping in order to find a car that best suits their needs and limited incomes.

C. California farmers producing agricultural goods that are exported to foreign countries. A good portion of these exports are bought by countries that export cars to the United States.

D. Stockholders and workers in United States companies that deal in imports and exports. For example, a salesperson for a car dealership that sells cars imported from Europe.

From *Personal Decision Making: Focus on Economics*, © National Council on Economic Education, New York, NY